Alain Mabanckou was born in 1966 in Congo. He currently lives in Los Angeles, where he teaches literature at UCLA. He was awarded the prestigious Grand Prix de Littérature Henri Gal for his body of work. He has also received the Subsaharan African Literature Prize for *Blue-White-Red*, and the Prix Renaudot for *Memoirs of a Porcupine*, which is published by Serpent's Tail along with his other novels, *Black Bazaar*, *Broken Glass* and *African Psycho*.

Praise for Alain Mabanckou

'Alain Mabanckou addresses the reader with exuberant inventiveness in novels that are brilliantly imaginative in their forms of storytelling. His voice is vividly colloquial, mischievous and often outrageous as he explores, from multiple angles, the country where he grew up, drawing on its political conflicts and compromises, disappointments and hopes. He acts the jester, but with serious intent and lacerating effect' Man International Booker Prize judges' citation

'Africa's Samuel Beckett ... Mabanckou is a subversive ... [his] freewheeling prose marries classical French elegance with Paris slang and a Congolese beat' *Economist*

'A dizzying combination of erudition, bawdy humour and linguistic effervescence' *Financial Times*

'Scorching wit and flights of eloquence ... vitriolic comedy and pugnacious irreverence' Boyd Tonkin, *Independent*

'A novelist of exuberant originality ... [*Tomorrow I'll Be Twenty* is a] delightful comic novel in which the boy narrator's ingenuousness is teamed with a sly authorial wit ... its seductive charm and intelligence recentre the world' Maya Jaggi, *Guardian*

'Mabanckou's novels about life in Africa have won much acclaim. *Tomorrow I'll Be Twenty*, a fictionalised account of his childhood in Congo-Brazzaville, is perhaps his best yet ... Nobel laureate JMG Le Clézio likens Mabanckou to Céline, Chinua Achebe, JD Salinger and Réjean Ducharme. Such a varied list suggests that he is, in fact, incomparable' *Financial Times*

'[*African Psycho* is] *Taxi Driver* for Africa's blank generation ... a deftly ironic Grand Guignol, a pulp fiction vision of Frantz Fanon's *The Wretched of the Earth* that somehow manages to be both frightening and self-mocking at the same time' *Time Out* New York

'[*Memoirs of a Porcupine*] subverts stereotypical notions of African literature, setting cliché and shibboleths on collision course. Magical realism meets black comedy in an excellent satire by an inventive and playful writer' *Herald*

THE
LIGHTS
OF
POINTE-
NOIRE

ALAIN MABANCKOU

Translated by Helen Stevenson

This book has been selected to receive financial assistance from English PEN's 'PEN Translates!' programme supported by Arts Council England. English PEN exists to promote literature and its understanding, uphold writers' freedoms around the world, campaign against the persecution and imprisonment of writers for stating their views, and promote the friendly co-operation of writers and free exchange of ideas. *www.englishpen.org*

Supported using public funding by **ARTS COUNCIL ENGLAND**

A complete catalogue record for this book can be obtained from the British Library on request

First published as *Lumieres de Pointe-Noire* in 2013 by Editions du Seuil, Paris

First published in the UK in 2015 by Serpent's Tail,
an imprint of Profile Books Ltd
3 Holford Yard
Bevin Way
London
WC1X 9HD
www.serpentstail.com

ISBN 978 1 84668 980 2
eISBN 978 1 78283 038 2

Designed and typeset by sue@lambledesign.demon.co.uk
Printed and bound in Italy by L.E.G.O. S.p.A. - Lavis (TN)

10 9 8 7 6 5 4 3 2 1

Contents

Now the hours are ripening
On the go-home tree
Meanwhile a drowsy numbness
longs for eyelids
heavy with a dust of regret

a child will be born long ago

First week

The miracle woman

For a long time I let people think my mother was still alive. I'm going to make a big effort, now, to set the record straight, to try to distance myself from this lie, which has only served to postpone my mourning. My face still bears the scars of her loss. I'm good at covering them over with a coat of fake good humour, but suddenly they'll show through, my laughter breaks off and she's back in my thoughts again, the woman I never saw age, never saw die, who, in my most troubled dreams, turns her back on me, so I won't see her tears. Wherever I find myself in the world, it takes just the cry of a cat alone at night, or the barking of dogs on heat, and I'll turn my face to the stars, recalling a tale from my childhood, of the old woman we thought we could see in the moon, carrying a heavy basket on her head. We kids would point her out just with a tilt of the nose, a lift of the chin, convinced we mustn't point at her or utter the slightest sound, or we'd wake next morning and find we'd been struck deaf or blind, or even with elephantitis or leprosy. We knew, of course, that the miracle woman had no quarrel with children and that the dread diseases she could inflict on peeping toms were punishments reserved for adults who tried to glimpse her naked when she went for a swim up there in the river of clouds. These perverts were encouraged by a handful of charlatans who said that if you saw the old woman without her clothes on it brought blessings on your business and good luck in your everyday life. Now we never really expected things to go all that well, which is probably why we closed our eyes, lying there in the damp grass, so she wouldn't think we were after the same thing as the grown-ups. She must have had a good laugh to herself up there, reading our innermost thoughts and detecting our every movement, thanks to her perfect ear. She'd turn around, look left, look right, then vanish the second we lay down on our stomachs and pretended to be asleep. We knew she was close by, she was watching us, and maybe she too enjoyed the game, which to us was a bit like hide-and-seek.

Then she'd reappear, we'd see her now, side on, like a shadow puppet, wrapped in layers of dense cloud. We watched her slow progression, transfixed, as a shower of shooting stars fell from her basket, like a firework display to launch the evening drum roll across the land. At that very moment I expect a child was being born somewhere, not knowing it owed its life to this woman, bent double by her penance, but guarantor of all life here below. And at the same time, as a calm fell upon the vault of heaven and at last the moon left the sky, a handful of stars suddenly switched off like lights, as though they'd been hit by bullets from the gun of a hunter standing behind us. We looked at each other, sadly. Someone, somewhere, had died. We knelt down, chin to chest, and mumbled: 'May his soul rest in peace...'

Who was this nomad of the nights of full moon, whose face no man or woman had ever seen? Some said her story went back to a time when the Earth and the Sky were always squabbling. The Earth said the Sky was faithless and fickle, had mood swings, yelled and roared, while the Sky said the Earth was mindless and dull. God was required to judge between them, and sided with the Sky, since He lived there. And so the miracle woman laid down her life, and took upon herself the sins born of the heedlessness of man. Through this act, she averted a disaster that would have brought about the extermination of the entire human race. During the season before this sacrifice of propitiation, famine and drought on an unprecedented scale came to several villages in the southern Congo. The animals were dying off and so much of the flora vanished that even the most optimistic sorcerers began to predict, within the next quarter-year, the disappearance of the Mayombe forest and the implacable advance of the desert, in which all would perish. That year, bush meat was a distant memory. People ate anything, just to survive, and some villagers made fortunes trading lizards, lightning bugs, ants, beetles, flies and mosquitoes. Within two months these all-invading creatures had completely vanished. There was a rumour that in certain tribes, when someone died, they fought over the body to be sure of at least one whole week of food.

The destruction of our land was foretold by a blind enchantress with a rasping voice and two crippled legs, who shuffled around on her butt. She revealed that the very hands of Time would forget our district, that in the coming days they would stop at midnight, and people would wake on the morning of that terrible moment to a new order of existence: scarcity, or complete absence of water, increased incidence of mirages, sandstorms and deadly heat waves. At first no one took these predictions very seriously. Everyone just said the blind and crippled sorceress was a victim of her own delusions, how else could you explain that each night she'd sell bananas, in front of her property, and though no one ever bought them, they still all disappeared? Where did she find them, when the desert had devoured over half the southern territory? She had more and more customers every day, but where did they all come from? This was in fact the start of the illusions; the sorceress's wares were the fruit of people's imagination.

A week after what became known as 'the Announcement', the first signs of the end of time began to appear. The birds had gone from the sky, leaving an empty abyss, a sign of a divine anger which even the cleverest sorcerers, powerless in the face of their panoply of limp, unresponsive amulets, could not fathom. These sages came together in a plenary session and took a decision that caused a general uproar: a woman must be 'handed over' to appease the divine wrath, and take on her own head the burden of human sin. According to this august assembly, men did not possess this redeeming power, God had only given it to women. The women took this verdict as an insult, and most of the young women shrank from the idea, saying their job was to ensure the line of descent. So that left only the older women. But they said, just because they had reached the twilight of their existence didn't mean they must accept a sacrifice devised for them by a bunch of old guys using their so-called knowledge of the world of darkness to camouflage their own cowardice. What did they stand to gain, anyway, their lives were nearly over, why should they sacrifice themselves for a happiness they'd never see? While the men and women were arguing it out, the situation got worse. The desert had by now absorbed a good part of the Mayombe forest and was heading off at full pelt towards the country's heartland. Seeing the country was in a state of breakdown, the miracle woman came down from her cabin perched up on the mountain top, and turned up uninvited in front of the wise men. On the night of a full moon, four sages from the village of Louboulou, and all its sorcerers, dragged her off, far away, into what was still left of the bush. Her hands were tied behind her back with strands of creeper. To some she was a scapegoat, to some a victim who died for the sins of others. They treated her roughly and abused her, which showed how deep was the community's belief that she had caused all the bad luck that had hit the region. No longer just a willing sacrifice, she was now truly guilty, and had given herself up, and in some people's eyes that was sufficient, they grabbed their whips, gritted their teeth, and lashed her. Stoically, she stood firm, and walked her Way of the Cross.

In time they came to a waterhole, though it was so small it would probably dry up in a few hours. The moon was full, just brushing the tops of the drought-withered trees. The Eye in the Sky had decided to witness this settling of human scores, so it shed its light upon the scene, until one of the sorcerers, in a quavering voice, began to read out the accusation, decreeing that in the public interest the old woman must live inside the luminous disc from now on and carry a basket on her head till the end of time; unprotesting, the sacrificed woman knelt down in the middle of the waterhole, her hands still bound, and raised her head to the sky. She made not a sound as one of the sorcerers stepped forward with a knife raised above his head. A deathly silence fell, as the sorcerer, with one single, swift and decisive movement, slit the woman's throat. At once the moon vanished, and did not reappear until the following month, with this time, trapped inside it, an old woman carrying a basket on her head. The southerners were amazed at the sight.

It was decreed that the first Friday of every new year should be the festival of the Sacrifice, when homage would be paid to the old woman. The birds reappeared in our sky, rain fell for a whole week, the harvest brought forth fruit once more, the rivers ran high and teemed with fish, and the animals went forth and multiplied till the bush was crawling with every imaginable species…

I'm grown up now, but belief remains intact, protected by a kind of reverence that resists the lure of Reason. And returning to my roots after twenty-three years away, I feel my faith more than ever. At every full moon anxiety takes hold of me, and pulls me out of doors. Everywhere I see the outline of things, like shadows watching me, surprised to see I'm not paying homage to the miracle woman. And I look up at the sky and I think that maybe the old bohemian has found eternal rest and been replaced by another woman, a bit younger than her, the woman I know best and who would have accepted the sacrifice too, the woman who brought me into the world, Pauline Kengué, who, I will say it, and write it now, to clear up any confusion, died in 1995…

The woman from nowhere

My mother left me with the enduring memory of her light brown eyes. I had to peer down deep into those eyes to catch sight of her worries; she had a way of keeping them from me, through a sudden contraction of her pupils. For her it was a defensive impulse, and for me was one explanation, among others, for why I felt that throughout my childhood she never looked me straight in the eye. I mistrusted her sudden joyful outbursts, which, deep down, concealed her sorrows, and presented me with a distorted image of my mother, as someone well armoured against the frustrations of daily life. I tried to see her more cowardly actions as the sign of inner suffering, but each time I came up against the same mask of serenity she wore every day of her brief existence. It would have been the height of dishonour for her to show me her vulnerability. In almost everything she did, she had one single purpose: to prove to me that with the blessing of our ancestors there was no difficulty on earth she could not overcome, like the time she dreamed that her mother, N'Soko, now deceased, had buried five hundred thousand CFA francs in the sand on the Côte Sauvage, so she went down there at sunrise with her eyes half closed and her hair still wild about her head. There, by chance, she found the stash of money, which made it possible for her to go back into business. Or when she got back from

[handwritten marginalia: a matriarch (patriarch shifted?) cultural standards of]

the Grand Marché on a day when things hadn't gone well, she'd distract me, sending me off to buy a litre of petrol, some spare wicks for the two Luciole storm lamps, then shut herself up in her room, and go back over her accounts. She didn't notice I was back again, and could hear her still murmuring prayers, blowing her nose and saying my grandmother's name, over and over, her words interspersed with sobbing. I knew it wasn't the bad day that had done this to her, it was the presence of the scary straw-hatted scarecrow behind the bedroom door. To me he felt like a human, watching us, moving about. His rags looked like strands of tangled creeper, waving around when you entered the room. My mother had been there when he was made, in Louboulou, the day Grandmother N'Soko, finding her maize plantation half ravaged by an army of persistent birds, had placed it in the middle of her field to protect the crops. Years later, when my grandmother died, Maman Pauline was determined she should inherit this object, while her brothers and sisters, baffled by her insistence, and by her disregard for material goods, had made a grab for the cattle and the plantation and sold them, since none of them wanted to set themselves up in the bush.

My orders were not to go near the scarecrow unless my mother said I should. She didn't really need to tell me, since I was already terrorised by the fact of its existence, and I couldn't understand what use he could be in our home. I would start shaking whenever, before a test or end-of-year exam, my mother would make me go and salute him, before setting off to school. Seeing me shrink from the bogeyman, she'd reassure me, saying, 'He'll bring you good luck, he'll tell you what to write to get a good mark.'

Whenever we moved house around the city, the scarecrow, who we called Massengo, came with us. When we'd rented in the Fonds Tié-Tié *quartier*, he'd been there, propped up behind the door of my parents' room. The year we lived with Uncle René, house-sitting while he was doing some training abroad, Massengo came too. When we bought our own place in the Voungou *quartier*, he stayed with us. Every New Year, my mother left a plate of pork and plantain bananas out for him, the traditional dish of the Bembé tribe. She talked to him for at least an hour to bring him up to date on what we'd done that year, and on our hopes and projects for the year just beginning. I learned later that my mother didn't have a bank account, that she kept her savings in a hole that was guarded by Massengo, who was said to have the power to increase tenfold all savings placed in his care. I believed this, especially as my mother was never without money…

For all the care she took to hide her worries from me, Maman Pauline could never quite conceal her fragility when, irritated that she still wouldn't look at me when I desperately tried to catch her eye, I would ask her whether anything was wrong. Or course then she'd immediately burst out laughing and tell me I was worrying for nothing, of course she was fine, she must be, she was laughing, a person with worries wouldn't be relaxed, or happy, like she was. She'd round off her little charade by adopting a manner too studiously relaxed to be genuine, and telling me some rambling story, still with that ill-contained hilarity that increased my anxiety and convinced me she was worried about something.

If my attention drifted off, she'd notice straight away:

'Why aren't you laughing too? Don't you like my story of the piglet born with two snouts and only one nostril? Don't you think it's funny?'

I didn't answer. I stared at the roof, then down at the floor. Now it was her turn to worry about me, as within seconds, as though it was catching, my face had suddenly darkened with the conviction that someone was out to harm her, or that, even with the magical powers of Massengo the scarecrow, she couldn't pay back the loan she'd taken out to buy a licence at the Grand Marché and work with an easy conscience. Aged eleven I was already aware that the market tax had broken up many families, with mothers in despair because they'd been banned from selling peanuts for being a bit late with their payments. They'd arrive in the morning to find some council workers standing, Cerberus-like, at their table. Negotiation was not a term they used. They were paid to evict traders and replace them with others who had given them a bribe. Either the traders paid with money they borrowed from others, or they went back home wondering how they were going to feed the kid sitting waiting for them, blissfully unaware of its mother's troubles. Now my mother wasn't in either of these categories, she was careful to pay the licence fee in time.

Her air of sadness had its origins elsewhere, and that look of hers, though not hard, not snake-like, even when she was angry, was the expression of her determination to scale the endless steps that rose before her, this humble peasant woman from Louboulou, a small town with red earth, that produced corn, and tubers and yams, and bananas, and grazing pigs. She wanted to forget that place, where the man due to be her husband ran off without a word, abandoning her to her fate a few months before my birth. So she chose to live as a woman from nowhere, amid the hurly-burly of the town of Pointe-Noire, where I am now, a coastal city with not much indulgence for people arriving with the soil of the fields on their feet. She looked on me as an extension of her existence, the ray of hope at the end of an infinitely long tunnel. I was the indisputable sign of the immortality she imagined she would finally achieve the day I emerged from her womb in a run-down building in the maternity hospital in the Mouyondzi district, that both torrid and glacial night of 24 February 1966, while the moon struggled to lighten the darkness and the cocks were already crowing at the new dawn. Scarcely able to believe her own happiness, which even the memory of the disaster with my father could not spoil, she anxiously placed her feverish hands on my chest to check I was still breathing, that I wasn't an apparition who would vanish the moment she turned her back. She had to be persuaded to let the nurse wash the newborn babe she cradled in her arms. All that because she feared I would take the same path as my two older sisters, who died at birth. She had never been able to solve the mystery of their premature departure. Perhaps the two angel children had heard the prediction of a cousin of our mother's, who, goaded by jealousy, had publicly declared one day that the destiny of Maman Pauline was the darkest of all her line. The same bad-mouthed cousin also said that my mother would have no children, that she'd die all alone in a hut, and if by any chance she did manage to have a baby, it would be a boy, an ungrateful boy who would leave the country when he was twenty years old, and be living thousands of kilometres away the day she drew her last breath. This baby would not belong to her, he would just be passing through, taking the first empty womb he could find.

But my mother swept aside these predictions, putting them down to her barren cousin's envy of another's fertility, and came to Pointe-Noire with a child in her arms, and the scarecrow of my grandmother, N'Soko, wrapped up in palm leaves. She walked with her pagne wrapped around her hips, a way of showing that, even in despair, her head was high. Her path was long and winding, till one day a new man appeared before her. He would become my father, my real father, as I saw it, the one I instinctively stretched out my little hands to, smiling at last as I felt myself swept up off the ground, defying gravity, carried by the invincible, unsurpassable physical strength of this man, landing high up on his shoulders, my legs gripping tight round his neck. That was the day I first pronounced those two resonant, magical, identical syllables, the vowels interlaced with the two twin consonants: 'papa'. This is the man I called deferentially 'Papa Roger', in my autobiographical book *Tomorrow I'll Be Twenty*, and who now lies in the Mont-Kamba cemetery, in a tomb close by my mother's…

Live and become

heard my mother had died in 1995. I was a student and had been living in a small studio in the 9th arrondissement of Paris, in the Rue Bleue, for over six years. I was expected back in Pointe-Noire for the funeral and the telephone rang endlessly. A cousin urged me to come back. My aunt Dorothée threatened to kill herself if I didn't show up. My cousin Kihouari yelled that we'd be cursed if I didn't get on the next plane.

I stopped picking up the phone. It was as though the news had paralysed me, and this pleading from thousands of kilometres away pushed me farther into my corner. The world felt too small, and time seemed to have stopped in its tracks. Even when I climbed the stairs of our apartment block I would go on up past my studio, and find myself on the sixth floor, though I lived on the second.

I didn't go.

The truth was, I dreaded coming face to face with the body of the woman I had last seen smiling, full of life. My fear of seeing her again, lifeless, had its roots in my childhood. Back then, like many other children of my age, I was phobic about corpses, especially since they were laid out in the yard so anyone who wished to could come and pay their last respects. Everyone had to file past the deceased, lean over them to within a few millimetres, and murmur some words of farewell. This proximity filled us children with dread, especially since, to our minds, the dead at first wandered on earth for a few weeks, waiting for their final departure, haunting the living, especially the children who had seen them during the funeral rites. Why them? Because the dead needed their innocence to survive the few days leading up to their departure.

We dreaded the hearse, too, we hated black. As it crossed the street we closed our eyes, convinced that the dead person was peering out at us through the windscreen, memorising our faces. Some of us trembled, pissing ourselves with fright, unable to speak for several days. The dreams of others were full of the deceased, their delirious nights haunted by people with horns, vampire teeth and long tails, as in the familiar representations of the Devil. I stopped going to the funeral wakes in our neighbourhood. Seeing someone lying inert, made up and scented with Mananas – the perfume of choice on these occasions – with their arms crossed, affected me so badly I'd dwell on it for weeks, convinced I would meet the ghost of the departed after nightfall.

Even though this time the deceased was my mother, I still couldn't control my fears and even made out to myself that shortage of funds for the journey home was a good enough alibi for getting out of it without feeling guilty. I couldn't bear to look at myself in the mirror, for fear I would find there the reflection of my ingratitude towards the woman who must be patiently waiting for me, in her coffin, surrounded by members of the family, all of them disgusted at my absence.

All through that dreadful day, as I paced the room and wrote pages of my poetry collection *Vagabond Legends*, which I

*objectifying, stripping her of her name/
identity in order to cope*

dedicated to the dead <u>woman,</u> her words echoed over and over in my mind. I thought back to our last meeting, in 1989, a few hours before I left for France, where I was to study law in Nantes. She had come to say goodbye and had travelled over five hundred kilometres to Brazzaville, where I had spent the last week.

We sat face to face in a bar in the Moungali neighbourhood, not far from the War Veterans building. Her expression was grim, her voice hoarse with emotion. She could scarcely string two words together. I held her in my arms and heard her call me 'papa', her way of showing me her affection. There was a moment's silence, then I saw her tears…

When she was able to speak again, she began to talk about the concerts given by our national orchestra, Les Bantous de la Capitale, in the 1960s, and the band Les Trois Frères, namely Youlou Mabalia, Loko Massengo and Michel Boyibanda.

'That was the golden age,' she said; 'we wore miniskirts and high heels and the men went round in bell-bottomed trousers and Salamander shoes. Pointe-Noire was famous for its atmosphere, and everyone had work. Even Zaireans started to arrive, though up till then you'd only see them in Brazzaville, which they reached from Kinshasa, crossing the River Congo…'

I nodded in agreement, and she went on:

'The atmosphere's gone now, there's no music, young people don't sing now, they just make noise. Anyway, I've stopped listening to their music, it gives me migraines…'

The waiter passed by our table, his trousers worn and ripped. My mother glowered at him, her mouth drawn tight with scorn:

'People don't dress properly these days! Look at that young man serving our drinks, what way is that to dress? This country's on its knees, I tell you! You're right to get out, leave all this behind you…'

The point of these digressions was simply to lessen the pain of separation, and help us forget we would be apart for a very long time. This was the bar where she always arranged to meet me when she came up from Pointe-Noire for her business. I was in my first years of university and was living in Brazzaville in a studio shared with my cousin Gilbert Moukila. When she turned up we were always relieved to see her: she'd give us a bit of money, so we didn't have to wait for the state grant, which got doled out only in tiny doses and was in any case barely sufficient for our needs. She gave each of us the same sum, thirty thousand CFA francs, the equivalent of our grant. It was enough to get us through to the end of one month and await the next one with no worries.

'So, you're off to France, then?' she said again, interrupting my thoughts, which had gone wandering off.

'Well, yes, I…'

'Oh, no need to apologise, Adèle was right!'

'Adèle?'

'My cousin, in Louboulou, the nasty gossip, who said I'd never have a child. I've often told you about her… I know you don't like to say her name.'

'But I *am* here! *I'm* your child!'

'I know, but this cousin also said that I'd probably only have one boy and that he would go off on a long journey, far from me, and I would die alone in a hut like a person who has no family… You're all I have in the world, but did you really love me?'

'Of course I did!'

'Oh, it doesn't matter, you're saying that to please me! It seems to me you're glad to be going to live with the Whites, you don't know how much you're hurting me, I didn't deserve this…'

'No, no, I'm not glad at all…'

'What will I do without you? Everyone will laugh at me because they'll see I'm all alone, do you see what I mean?'

She took a gulp of her beer and whispered:

'Why do they do this to me?'

Since I didn't know who she was talking about this time, I ventured:

'Who?'

'France! The Congo! They've plotted to steal my son away, my only reason for living! There are lots of children in this country, why not send them to France instead of you? Look at me sitting here now! I'm as good as dead...'

Resigned, she emptied the rest of her bottle into her glass, knocked it back in one, adjusted her headscarf.

'Don't you disappoint me, my boy. I've always been a model mother to you...'

She opened her handbag and took out a bundle of notes.

'There you are, that's everything I earned this month, you'll need it where you're going... I've got a few notes left over I can give to Gilbert.'

We'd been in the bar nearly an hour now. She had reeled off most of the names of people in our family who'd died. Uncle Albert, who worked for the National Electric Company. My deceased grandmother N'Soko, who saw me only once. Grandpa Grégoire Moukila, who was chief of the village of Louboulou, that far-flung corner of the Bouenza district, where all our family came from, and who lived to be a hundred and twelve. Not forgetting, of course, my two sisters, who'd died only a few hours after they came into this world.

'Don't forget them, the ones we've lost. And the day you

mem. of a porc. ? reference

can't see your own shadow, you'll know you've ceased to exist yourself…'

She was silent for a moment, then added: '…And then you'll be in the next world, like our ancestors who've passed on now, but still protect us, day and night…'

Outside, the day was starting to fade. Inside the café, I could barely make out my mother's features, only her eyes that glistened, lighting up the room. I could hear the frantic beating of her heart. The silence was like a wall between us, which neither one wished to break through. We said nothing, which said almost everything. She was transmitting something to me, but I didn't know what. I was careful not to speak. The slightest word would have ruined the moment.

She breathed out slowly, as though summoning up her courage, then got to her feet.

'Just don't disappoint me.'

She stood outside the entrance to the bar now, and I was behind her, like a shadow. In her eyes I could read what she hadn't dared say out loud: she had lost me, for good.

She hailed a taxi parked opposite the café. The vehicle cut across the street in the path of the oncoming traffic and braked in front of my mother, who dived inside, holding back her tears.

I stood there, at the door of the bar, like a pillar of salt.

She wound down the window:

'Become who you want to become and always remember this: hot water never forgets it used to be cold…'

The taxi shot off. I watched it go, weaving through the traffic towards the Ballon d'Or roundabout.

I would never see my mother again…

One thousand and one nights

For a long time, then, I let people think my mother was still alive. In a way I had no choice but to lie, having picked up the habit way back in primary school when I brought my two older sisters back to life in an attempt to escape the teasing of my classmates, who were all very proud of their large families, and offered to 'lend' my mother their offspring. Obsessed with the idea of bearing another child, she consulted the town's most noted doctors, as well as most of its traditional healers, who claimed to have treated women who'd been sterile for twenty years or more. Disappointed in the white men's medicine, and cheated by the crooks in the backstreets of Pointe-Noire, who had never healed so much as a scratch with their spells and sorcery, my mother resolved to accept her condition: mother of a single child, she told herself there were other women on this earth who had no children at all, and would have been delighted to be in her shoes. But she still couldn't just sweep aside the fact that the society she lived in considered a woman with one child as pitiful as a woman who had none. Similarly, an only son was a pariah. He was the cause of his parents' misfortune, having 'locked' his mother's belly behind him, so he could be an only one, enjoying this lowly distinction which the community scorned. He was also said to have special powers: he could make it rain, he could stop the rain, bring fever on his enemies, and prevent their wounds from healing. He was all but assumed to have power over the rotation of the earth.

I was quite prepared to believe all this, and searched in vain for the hidden powers I was thought to possess, finally concluding that what an only child really possessed was the secret fortune to be gained from his parents' constant fear they might lose him. The parents were convinced that he belonged to another world, he was bored in theirs and that all the toys in the world could never make up for that boredom. The sisters I resuscitated in their entirety became my only armour, reliable characters in an imaginary world where I felt at ease and where, for once, I could act like an adult, and not depend on others to take care of me.

When I mentioned my sisters to my friends, I probably exaggerated. I proudly made out they were tall, beautiful, intelligent. I confidently added that they wore rainbow-coloured dresses and spoke most languages known on earth. And if anyone doubted me, I'd tell them they rode round in a red Citroën DS convertible, driven by their hired boy, that they'd flown in planes more times than they could count, and had sailed across seas and oceans. I knew I'd scored a point when the questions began:

'So, have you been in the Citroën DS with your sisters?' asked the most outspoken of my playmates, his eyes gleaming with envy.

Quickly I found the perfect alibi:

'No, I'm too small, but they've promised they'll let me when I'm as tall as them…'

Another, spurred by jealousy, I expect, would counter:

'You're making it up! Since when did you have to be big to get in a car? I've seen kids smaller than us in cars!'

I kept my cool:

'Yeah, but was it in a Citroën DS you saw them?'

'Um, no … a Peugeot…'

'Well, there you go! To get in a Citroën DS convertible you have to be bigger than us because it's a really fast car, it's dangerous if you're still little…'

No one in the group of kids had ever seen these sisters, and as my mythomania grew, so did their disbelief, and their questions rained down on me like gunfire. They were in Europe, I said, in America, or maybe Asia, they'd come back for a holiday in the dry season.

'Can we meet them? Will they play with us?' they all chorused.

'Of course, I'll introduce them to you, but they're too big to play with us.'

Caught in the web of my own fictions, I started to believe in them more than my friends did, and I awaited the return of my siblings with quiet confidence. I kept a lookout for planes, tracked every Citroën DS in town, and to my great despair, found not a single convertible. The day I did see one, my disappointment was huge: it was black, and driven by a white couple with no child on board…

I was heard talking to myself on the way to school or in our neighbourhood, when my mother sent me to buy salt or paraffin. I'd spent so much time with my sisters in my head that now I saw them opening the door of the house at night, coming inside, going through to the kitchen, rooting among the pans and the leftovers of the food my mother had made. One day I whispered to my mother that my sisters had come to see us and found nothing to eat; she was silent for a moment, then, as though she found all this quite normal and was surprised I had only just noticed their nocturnal visits, she said:

'Have you never noticed I leave two full plates out every evening, at the entrance to the house?'

'I thought they were for Miguel…'

She tried not to laugh:

'No, they're not for the dog, though he does sometimes finish what your sisters leave.'

'One of them had a yellow dress on and the other had a green blouse…'

'Shush! Don't tell anyone, not even your father, or they'll stop coming…'

The day after this conversation my mother left out two dishes of beef and beans with two glasses of orange juice. I stood behind her to make sure she gave the sisters the same food as I'd had and that my older siblings each got the same amount, so they wouldn't squabble. If I thought one had more than the other I would move a piece of meat over to the other plate, to even things up, while my mother looked on with a small smile of satisfaction.

In the morning I rushed out of the door to find that the two plates were still in the same place where my mother had left them. My sisters hadn't touched their food. I shouted to Maman Pauline just as she was coming out of her room:

'They haven't eaten!'

'Yes they have…'

'The food's still on the plates!'

'Well, yes, it would be… It looks to you like there's food on these plates, but in fact there's nothing there. They're empty.'

'But I can see there's food on them!'

At this, as though anxious to cut short this conversation, which could have continued for some time, she asked:

'If there's food on these plates, then tell me this, why didn't Miguel eat it?'

'I don't know but…'

'Dogs can see things that we can't. Miguel knows there's nothing on the plates, your sisters have had a feast…'

One evening, I was delighted to be given an apple that my father had brought back from the Hotel Victory Palace where he worked as the receptionist. I decided to show my gratitude by revealing the secret of my sisters' apparitions.

'I swear it, I saw them with my own eyes, clear as I see you now, Papa! And, when they eat, us humans can't see that they've eaten, only dogs can! You do believe me, don't you?'

He listened to me calmly as I babbled on, even acting out my sisters' movements. When I'd finished my somewhat incoherent account, which he took for the ramblings of a rather over-talkative child, I felt bad for having said too much, and broken my pact with these two characters.

'Don't tell Maman I told you the secret. She'll be cross with me…'

I could tell he would talk to my mother about it because he didn't promise not to. All I got was a quick nod of the head before he went off to join my mother in the bedroom. I heard Maman Pauline's laughter, then, in a hushed voice, 'Don't laugh loud like that, he'll hear you…'

I had actually just lost the naivety which had made it possible for me to steer my way between the real world and the imaginary, to inhabit both without being paralysed by the wall of doubt which was a feature of the adult domain. I was sure I had lost the pleasure of talking with my sisters because I had not held my tongue. This made me terribly sad.

Those next few days, whenever I got up in the middle of the night to look out for my sisters, I found myself face to face with Miguel. His hair bristled and he quivered, pointing his nose towards the street, his way of telling me that the two people had just left, because they didn't want to talk to me now I had revealed their nocturnal presence to Papa Roger. I was angry with myself, and my attitude towards my father changed. I think it was at this time that I began to cultivate the art of silence, to tell myself that anything I said would only make things worse. I spoke less and less of my sisters to my friends, and they stopped asking me. It was all over, they knew that, it was time I became a normal kid again.

Sitting in front of the door to our house, I watched Miguel, who looked as teary-eyed and sad as I did. I no longer knew what he meant when he wagged his tail. I expect he was trying to comfort me. Maybe he could help me recapture the joy I'd got from thinking I too belonged in that other world, the one he sensed with his canine intuition, the instinct God gave him instead of the gift of speech, which he'd given humans.

To redeem myself in my sisters' eyes, I secretly ate the food my mother continued to leave out for them each night, by the door, and told myself that whatever went into my stomach also went into theirs. In the morning, my mother was astonished to find the empty plates, and would reprimand Miguel, who would turn to me with a look of red-eyed reproach. But when I gently stroked him he at once grew calm, for he alone understood the true depth of my sadness…

My father's glory

My father was a small man, two heads shorter than my mother. It was almost comic, seeing them walking together, him in front, her behind, or kissing, with him standing up on tiptoe to reach. To me he seemed like a giant, just like the characters I admired in comic strips, and my secret ambition was one day to be as tall as him, convinced that there was no way I could overtake him, since he had reached the upper limit of all possible human growth. I realised he wasn't very tall only when I reached his height, around the time I started at the Trois Glorieuses secondary school. I could look him straight in the eye now, without raising my head and waiting for him to stoop down towards me. Around this time I stopped making fun of dwarves and other people afflicted by growth deficiency. Sniggering at them would have meant offending my father. Thanks to Papa Roger's size I learned to accept that the world was made of all sorts: small people, big people, fat people, thin people.

He was often dressed in a light brown suit, even when it was boiling hot, no doubt because of his position as receptionist at the Victory Palace Hotel, which required him to turn out in his Sunday best. He always carried his briefcase tucked into his armpit, making him look like the ticket collectors on the railways, the ones we dreaded meeting on the way to school when we rode the little 'workers' train', without a ticket. They would slap you a couple of times about the head to teach you a lesson, then throw you off the moving train. The workers' train was generally reserved for railway employees, or those who worked at the maritime port. But to make it more profitable, the Chemin de fer Congo-Océan (CFCO) had opened it to the public, in particular to the pupils of the Trois Glorieuses and the Karl Marx Lycée, on condition they carried a valid ticket. As a result they became seasoned fare dodgers, riding on the train top, in peril of their lives. It was quite spectacular, like watching *Fear in the City* at the Cinema Rex, to see an inspector pursuing

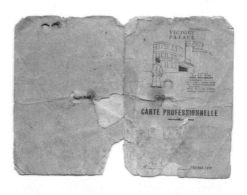

a pupil between the cars, then across the top of the train…

Papa Roger walked with a lively step, his eyes glued to his watch – which made my mother say he was the most punctual man on earth. With him everything was timed to the exact minute. He left the house at six in the morning, took the bus on the Avenue of Independence, opposite the Photo Studio Vicky, and arrived in the centre of town half an hour later.

At seven o'clock on the dot he was in the reception of the Victory Palace, straight as a rod, greeting the first clients of the day, as they made their way to the restaurant for breakfast. He stood at the desk and scanned from the hotel entrance to the street outside. As soon as he saw a new client getting out of a car, he shook a little bell. Two uniformed employees came running up to the main entrance, grabbed their suitcases and deposited them at reception. They then took them up to the upper floors after my father had filled out the registration forms and assigned them a room. He took a sly pleasure in describing this procedure to us at table in the evening. It was difficult for him to conceal a kind of pride which, in my mother's eyes, was nothing but bluster. He would stop in the middle of eating and crow:

'I'm the most important employee at that Victory Palace! It's me, no one else, who decides what room to put a client in! If they look like a jerk – you get a lot of them with these Europeans on holiday – I don't offer them the good room with the view of the garden. I keep that for the clients I like, the regulars who come back every year. Sometimes I might give someone a bad room to start off with, if I don't know them, and then if they're nice to me during their stay I'll switch them. They usually remember I've done that when they leave, and they'll give me a big tip!'

He got back from work at five in the evening, bringing a few French magazines, which he read at table after dinner, reacting out loud to what he read:

'What? Not possible! I don't believe it! Why on earth did they do that? The French are mad!!'

At the weekend he wore white pyjamas with red stripes, and brown slippers that were too big for his feet. They were a present, he reminded us, from his boss, Mme Ginette.

'Even if they were too small for me, I'd wear them, a present's a present! They're called *charentaises*, no one else in this town has them! They're so splendid, I know people who'd wear them to go walking round town in, if they had a pair! But they're meant for staying at home in, and reading the paper. That's what they do in Europe!'

He'd sit down on the doorstep in the morning, and continue his perusal of the newspapers that sat in a pile next to him, with a stone on top, to stop them blowing away in the wind. He forgot to drink the coffee my mother set down just next to him, concentrating on turning the pages, turning back to something he'd read a few minutes before and grabbing a red pen to scrawl on it. Then he'd suddenly break off reading, glance over at me, and notice I was sitting there under the mango tree with my jaw dropping in admiration.

'You want to read with me? Come on, then!'

I'd dash over to him, having waited impatiently for this moment. He read to me what he called the 'world news'. I quickly learned the more complicated names of foreign countries and their leaders. Europe, America, Asia or Oceania ceased to feel like distant lands. I noticed my father used his red pen to underline the more difficult French words.

'I'll check those words on Monday in the dictionary at the

Victory Palace… I need to learn them so I can use them at the right moment with the clients.'

Picking out two more, and underlining them irritably, I heard him grumble:

'I don't understand why people don't write simply, why they have to write words no one understands! *Antediluvian*, for example, or *apocryphal*, what's that mean?'

Indignantly, he turned the page. Here was the world news. He looked displeased as he grumbled:

'For goodness' sake, the French are crazy! Why don't they talk about what's happening in our country? We've had a *coup d'état* here, and there's not one line about it! President Marien Ngoubai was murdered last week! The French are in league with them, they must be, they can't possibly not mention it! The French are behind the whole thing!'

Seeing I said nothing, he went on:

'I'll tell you something, my boy, now you listen to Roger! They don't talk about us because our country's too small! And because it's too small, people forget about it, and think it's only other countries that have mosquitoes, and poverty and civil wars. Not true! We've got every problem there is here, you only have to look around you! It's always the same, in the sea people only think about the sharks and the whales, because they make all the noise! No one thinks about the small fry who are just there to get eaten by the big fish!'

My mother became aware of my increasing fascination with Papa Roger and his reading, and began to get a little jealous. As soon as my father was gone she grabbed hold of the newspaper and withdrew to a corner of the yard with her back to a mango tree, saying:

'Don't disturb me, I'm reading!'

She looked like *Reading Woman* by Jean-Honoré Fragonard. How had she managed to hide from me for so long that she knew how to read? She concentrated hard, checking out of the corner of her eye that, like my father, she had my attention.

The next time this happened, I went over to her and realised she was holding the newspaper upside down. I pointed this out to her with a mocking smile. Unruffled by what she perceived to be an insult, she looked me up and down, returned the mocking smile and said:

'Do you really think that I, Pauline Kengué, daughter of Grégoire Moukila and Henriette N'Soko, am so crazy I'd read a paper upside down? I did it deliberately to see your reaction! Don't you go thinking you and your father are the only ones in this house who know how to read and write!'

On the outside, nothing has changed, apart from the air-conditioners fitted above the windows and the satellite dishes on the roof. Built in the late 1940s, in the centre of town, a short distance from the Côte Sauvage and the railway station, the Victory Palace is one of the oldest hotels in Pointe-Noire. In 1965, the first owner, M. Trouillet, handed over the management to Ginette Broichot, and she bought it from him in 1975. Since it was first erected, the building has watched from a distance as new constructions go up around it, and with slight arrogance preserves the typical structure of that time, concrete, with a huge white façade at the corner of Rue Bouvanzi and Avenue Bolobo.

I don't dare enter the building, as though I fear my father's ghost might be lurking somewhere, resenting this return to his past, which is also, indirectly, my own. I recall how he used to boast that he was the doyen of this hotel, and the most loyal member of its staff. The proof of this lay in his special treatment by Mme Ginette, who never raised her voice to him, while the rest of the staff lived in fear of the wrath of the French boss. Madame Pauline thought Papa Roger's monthly salary was twice what it really was, when in fact he was constantly asking for an advance or counting on getting tips from the clients. He had managed to get my maternal uncle, Jean-Pierre Matété, a job as a room boy. In the summer, Marius, one of my 'half-brothers', and I worked cleaning rooms and washing dishes. Sometimes, if she went back to France on holiday, Mme Ginette would put him in charge of the hotel. During these periods he stepped into the boss's shoes and ran the place with an iron fist. If anyone's uniform wasn't perfect he would tell them off, and he shouted at the gardener if he was late watering the plants. Papa Roger didn't mince his words, calling some people ignorant, others bastards, and writing their names down in his notebook so he could report back to Mme Ginette when the time came. The employees secretly longed for the boss to return as soon as possible, since being shouted at by a Negro was worse than being shouted at by a white.

I will never forget the time he fell into a deep gloom, when the stories he brought home from work, and which my mother and I adored, dried up. It turned out Mme Ginette's father had come over from France, and was staying at the Victory Palace indefinitely. My father was convinced that his boss had finally found a hidden way of imposing a ruthless inspector on the staff, and this he was not prepared to tolerate. An elderly, sharp-eyed man, he sat in the lobby all day long, watching what went on. Papa Roger claimed that his own role had been diminished, that the atmosphere of the hotel was being ruined by what he called 'the intruder'. Employees mustn't take anything home, not even an apple. Newspapers, which my father usually slipped into his bag when the whites had finished reading them, had to stay in the hotel, till eventually they were thrown out. The boss's father would openly stand behind a client so he could hear whether Papa Roger handled the conversation properly.

'Every day, he's there, watching us, he tells the *patronne* everything, and then she comes and ticks us off, like children! Is that the way to do things?' he'd ask my mother.

She'd stay quiet as a clam, and probably couldn't see why it bothered my father so much. Then, feeling she ought to say something, she just mumbled:

'Well, after all, it is his daughter's hotel... So it's his hotel too!'

'Oh right, so what are we, then? Was it him that gave me the job or his daughter? Anyway, it won't last long, we're going to sort him out next week...'

The plan, inspired by my father, in collusion with several employees, was carried out on Monday morning, after heated discussion the previous day, during which they had to convince a few cowards who thought if they went this far they might be sacked without pay. But what really mattered to my father was his territory. He would rather be sacked than submit each morning to the watchful eye of the 'intruder'.

They discreetly brought a plant into the Victory Palace known as '*kundia*'. It had powerful spikes, invisible to the naked eye. Seen through a microscope, they looked like rows of bristling needles, which came away on contact with a foreign body. Farmers used them round the edges of their fields to stop animals or thieves taking the fruit of their crops. If it accidentally brushed your skin, the only thing to do was resist the temptation to scratch for as long as possible, because the more you scratched, the deeper the teeth of the *kundia* dug into your skin, and the agony could last for an hour or more.

One of my father's sidekicks put on a pair of gloves and scattered the *kundia* bristles on the 'intruder's' armchair. Papa Roger's role, from this point on, was to make sure no one but the intruder sat there.

The old man came down from his room in his bermudas around ten in the morning. First he did his round of the restaurant, examining each table, straightening a chair he judged out of line, or giving orders to the waiters. Only once he had completed his tour, which for him had become a tradition, and for the employees a form of torture, did he finally take his breakfast.

Half an hour later, he sank into his armchair in the lobby, sprawled out with his legs stretched in front of him, his hands resting on his stomach, eyes closed. This relaxed attitude lasted no more than a few seconds.

'There are red ants in here! Red ants in my chair!'

He scratched desperately at his legs, then at his hands, and his face. He yelled for someone to bring him a drink of water. The staff clustered round him, till Mme Ginette, drawn by the noise, appeared from the stairs, horrified:

'Quick, get him to hospital! It's a tropical infection!'

The ambulance siren could be heard already outside and the victim was assisted by three employees, who all, for the first time ever, were wearing gloves.

That was the last time the 'intruder' was seen hanging around the lobby. Papa Roger had recovered his territory and at home we could tell, because he started telling stories about the Victory Palace again...

Quickly I walk away from the hotel, because someone's been watching me from inside for a while now. Perhaps he thinks I'm a potential client trying to choose between his hotel and the competitor, the Atlantic Palace, only two hundred metres away.

Mme Ginette is no longer the owner, she sold the hotel to the Congolese in 1985, and went back to France. She's in her nineties now. Once I ran into her niece in Montpellier, and we've stayed in touch.

The woman next door

The man I called my father died in 2005, ten years after Maman Pauline. I am not sure I ever really knew him. We were both intimate and distant. Intimate, because I had always felt his eyes watching me, accompanying me every step of the way, anxious I might stumble or fall, concerned I should choose the path he had opened up for me.

He seemed distant, too, not because he wasn't my biological father, but because I knew nothing about him, never having met a single member of what I might have considered my 'paternal family', even if, to do him justice, his relationship with my mother had never been sealed at the *mairie*. Their union was an unspoken agreement, made material by the fact that a man and a woman lived under the same roof with a child, in a society where the collective opinion was more important than any signature on a piece of paper, or vows before a public authority. Sometimes, even when a civil marriage had taken place, a few wise old men would mutter among themselves:

'So what, they just want to be like white people, those papers don't count in our eyes, what matters is the word of the ancestors, they don't need papers, people tear them up, anyway, after a few months' marriage. Can the word of the ancestors be torn up?'

No, my parents were not officially married. In fact he wasn't actually married to Maman Martine either, his other wife, with whom he had had eight children. This woman was what was called my mother's 'rival', the word 'rival' in the language of the Congolese meaning 'co-wife'. In itself, even the term 'co-wife' was incorrect, since neither of my two mothers had ever married Papa Roger before the mayor of Pointe-Noire. If it came to it, Maman Martine could claim more rights than my mother: she had had children with Papa Roger, her status of 'wife' had been legitimised by a traditional marriage, while in my mother's case, my father had settled it all by buying a drink for my mother's older brother, my maternal uncle, Albert.

I was aware of a generation gap between my 'two mothers'. There were two eras, one of which might be considered that of the black-and-white photo, the other that of experimentation with colour. The age difference between them was more than twenty years, enough to ensure they had different takes on life, different interests. In this respect, Papa Roger had done the same as many other polygamists in this country: he had thrown in his lot with a younger woman, a very young woman, in this case – my mother – to compensate for his first wife's declining beauty, and perhaps to protect himself against what he perceived as the monotony of married life, which they had shared now for nearly twenty years. But these were not the real reasons. Many polygamists needed their multiple marriages in order to feel strong and 'manly'. You certainly had to be financially comfortable to juggle two house-holds and bring up a brood so close in age that the names of some children got forgotten, or confused with others. In order to make ends meet, husbands usually sent their wives out to work, while they stayed at home or hung out in the local bars, where they might well meet another young lady to swell the ranks of the harem. Papa Roger, though a polygamist, was not of this breed; it was Maman Martine who stayed at home. She was more traditional, kept to the kitchen, often silent and self-effacing, speaking only in the language of her tribe, in *bembé*, not *munukutuba*, the language of Pointe-Noire, even though she had lived in this town for many years. She was the living embodiment of the 'village woman', who, it was said, expected her husband to provide everything for her. Whenever husband and wife argued, she would consult the council of old grey-beards, who welcomed the opportunity for a get-together and a good excuse to get drunk on palm wine, settling the dispute by the by. Maman Pauline, on the other hand, was more 'with it' – indeed, rather too much so for some people's tastes, going out when she felt like it, and walking into a bar full of men without any of the bowing and scraping they considered their due. She did this by way of provocation, and if you pointed it out she would reply:

'If they're so respectable, what are they doing hanging out in a bar while their wives are at home? Looking for other women?'

Her independence came from the groundnut and banana business she ran at the Grand Marché, and even more so from what she considered the great achievement of her life: the purchase of a plot of land in Pointe-Noire, in the Voungou district. My father didn't like her being autonomous, it made him feel, in his words, 'useless'. A woman shouldn't 'wear the trousers' in a relationship, or acquire possessions in her own name, these were the prerogatives of the husband, who also had the right to marry as many other women as he chose.

Much later – I must already have been at the lycée – Papa Roger started seeing another woman, one he intended to take as a third 'rival'. Usually he was the most punctual man on earth, but now he started coming home late to my mother's house, or to Maman Martine's, and making up excuses, contradicting himself, arousing the suspicion of his two 'official' wives. He'd tell Maman Martine he was a bit late because he'd stopped off at my mother's house. Then the next day, when he was meant to be sleeping at our house, he would argue that he had to go to Maman Martine's on some urgent business, which he didn't go into.

He couldn't play this game for much longer than a few weeks. Maman Martine got wind of the affair through one of her friends, and alerted my mother:

'I think Roger's seeing Célestine… he hasn't laid a finger on me for weeks, we're like strangers in bed. I know him, there's a woman on the scene.'

'No! Célestine? Can't he do better than that?'

Maman Martine, already half resigned to it, said meekly:

'Well, it doesn't matter much to me, I'm out of the running, I said goodbye to my youth a while back. But what's this Célestine got that you haven't? You're young, you're beautiful, you work hard, you and I have never fallen out! That Roger! He'll never change! Well, I'm just going to tell him to keep his hands off me till he's stopped seeing another woman on the side!'

My mother would have gone to the stake to prove my father's innocence. She was convinced it was only gossip, put about by jealous neighbours. But over the next few weeks my father's alibis grew less and less convincing, and my mother cornered him and demanded the truth.

Papa Roger raised his voice:

'Why are you and Martine spying on me? She won't let me sleep when I'm at her house, you won't let me breathe at yours, where *am* I meant to sleep? Tell me that!'

'Go and sleep at Célestine's! You might as well, I'm not

sharing my bed with you! Aren't two wives enough for you? You do nothing but snore when you are here! What am I meant to do? Find myself a lover?'

'Fine, if that's the way it is, I'm going out to get some air!'

'You do that! You go and find her!'

'That's enough, Pauline! Every day it's the same in this house! Is it because it's your house? If it was my house would you dare talk to me like that? I'm fed up with it, and if it carries on, I'm going home!'

I sometimes got the feeling in my mother's house that my father felt a bit like the lodger, since she was the one who had not only purchased the land but also built the house, which Papa Roger now visited every other day, alternating with his own home, a four-roomed house where Maman Martine lived with my eight half-brothers and -sisters.

The affair of the third wife eventually poisoned the atmosphere in both households. At ours, my parents no longer spoke to each other as they had. The slightest spark was enough to light the fire and set them off arguing, even though I was standing behind them, unable to understand why they were rowing about what seemed to me like the kind of things that occupy kids in the playground.

The situation grew worse every day, and in the end my mother and Maman Martine joined forces, and decided that it was up to us children to go and pay a little 'courtesy visit' to the potential 'co-wife'. Permission was even granted to sort her out by whatever means we saw fit.

I was part of the little group that set off on this punitive expedition, along with six of my half-brothers. One afternoon we went over to the neighbourhood where the woman lived, having been told her name by our mothers: Célestine. Outside her house we found a woman of a certain age, and Yaya Gaston, the oldest of us, spoke to her, saying:

'Excuse me, madame, we're looking for a young woman called Célestine, your daughter, we need to talk to her…'

The woman answered curtly:

'What do you want with her?'

I felt Yaya Gaston's body shake with anger, and he clenched his fist:

'Mind your own business, you old crone! We've come to tell your daughter to keep her little panties up and stop bothering our father, or we'll beat her up! She should be ashamed, stealing money from a respectable man with two families!'

'Well, go on, then. Beat me up!'

'We don't want you, old lady! We want to talk to Célestine! Come on, get out of the way, we need to search this place, we know she's hiding in there!'

She burst out laughing:

'There's only one Célestine here, and that's me! So what are you waiting for? Hit me!'

Yaya Gaston shrank back, turned to us and then looked at the woman again for a few seconds. Grey hair. Large, thick spectacles. Threadbare, patched pagnes. She must be older than Maman Martine, she could be Maman Pauline's grandmother.

'It's – you're – you're her?' stammered our big brother, incredulously, his fist still clenched as though he still meant to hit her.

'You want to see my ID or what? You just try to hit me, and you'll be cursed to the end of time!'

Gaston unclenched his fist and turned to us again:

'I can't. I just can't… She's really old. Who'll hit her for me?'

'I said hit me!' yelled the woman, commanding now, sure

none of us would dare lift a finger against an old woman.

Since no one in the group moved, and we were all looking at the ground, Yaya Gaston settled for intimidating the old woman:

'We've come to warn you! If you don't stop hanging round our father, you'll live to regret it! Even if you are... like you are!'

'And how am I? Old, am I? Stink do I? Do I ask your father to come over here? Go and sort out your own affairs, and tell your mothers to satisfy their man, because in my day, believe me, I was such a great lay, my late husband would forget to go to work for a whole month! And tell your mothers to look to their cooking, because when your father comes here you'd think he hadn't eaten in years! And now, if you don't get off my land, I'm going to expose myself to you. Then you'll see with your own eyes what your father's up to when he's not with your mothers! I've got white hairs on my pubis, you want to see them?'

Yaya Gaston was already out of her yard, with his fingers stuffed in his ears to block out her obscenities. We dashed after him, and fled with our tails between our legs, just as the old woman lifted her pagne around her waist to shake her arse at us.

'Don't look back, it brings bad luck!' Gaston cried.

Anyway, once Papa Roger heard about our visit from Célestine, he began to visit her less often, particularly since we started hiding out near by in the hope of catching him going into the house of the woman we considered a witch, who had cast a spell on our father.

A month went by and the 'affair' of the third wife was closed. Papa Roger returned to coming home on time, sitting in a corner to read the weekly magazines from Europe, and exclaiming at the idiot French for forgetting to mention our country, because it was only tiny...

Death at his heels

I never felt I really knew Papa Roger very well, partly because he told me nothing about his own parents. I didn't know whether they were alive, or had passed on into the next world. Nor had I ever set foot in Ndounga, his native village. This didn't bother me, as I cultivated a visceral hatred for anything connected to any paternal branch, my natural father having cleared off when my mother needed him. To me Papa Roger was father and grandfather, the perfect paternal rootstock, resistant to wind and weather, bringing forth fruit in every season. So I had given up desperately trying to find out about my paternal forebears.

I owe it to Papa Roger that my childhood was scented with the sweet smell of green apples. This was the fruit he brought home for me every week from the Victory Palace Hotel. In our town it was a great treat to eat an apple. For us it was one of the most exotic fruits to come from the colder regions. As I bit into it, I felt I was sprouting wings that would carry me far away. I'd sniff the fruit first, with my eyes closed, then munch it greedily, as though I was worried someone would suddenly come and ask me for a bite and spoil my pleasure in crunching it down to the last little pip, since no one had ever taught me how to eat an apple. Papa Roger stood there in front of me, smiling. He knew he could get me to do anything he wanted by simply giving me an apple. I'd suddenly turn into the most talkative boy on earth, even though I was by nature rather reserved. My mother realised the havoc an apple could wreak in my behaviour. She'd fly into one of her rages, usually at my expense, which to this very day tarnishes my pleasure in that delicious smell:

'There you go again, telling your father all sorts when you've eaten an apple! I'll start to think they're alcoholic, and have to ban them!!'

'I didn't do anything!'

'I see, so why did you tell him I went out with someone this afternoon, then? Don't come asking me to get your supper tonight! Let that be a lesson to you!'

It was true, I had been rather indiscreet that day, whispering to my father that a slim, tall man had dropped by our house, talked with my mother, after which the two of them had gone to a local bar for a drink. At this my father flew into a rage and yelled at my mother:

'I thought so! It's that guy Marcel, isn't it? You said it was all over between you and that imbecile! More fool me!'

My father refused to sit down at table with us that day, and shut himself up in the bedroom. Marcel was someone Maman Pauline had met around the same time she met my father, but she must have made the choice she did because Marcel was a seasoned womaniser who believed women fell at his feet because he had a great body. According to my mother, nothing happened between them. She took a fistful of earth in her right hand, scattered it in the air, which meant, in our tradition, that she swore she had told me the truth, the whole truth, nothing but the truth; you couldn't mess around with this custom, it had been used by our tribe since the dawn of time. Anyone who swore like this when in fact they'd been lying got a terrible headache the next day, and sometimes had to stay in bed for days on end. First they vomited, then their skin dried up. My mother did not develop any of these symptoms over the next few days. So I decided to believe her version, and let drop Papa Roger's, even though somewhere deep down I still wasn't sure.

Papa Roger was convinced Marcel was still after my mother and that something was going on between them, something lasting, perhaps, since he seemed to reappear every two or three years. When I was eight or nine years old, a really memorable fight broke out between the two men in the rue de Louboulu, in the Rex district. This was Uncle Albert's turf, he worked as a civil servant for the National Electricity Company and had been the first person on my mother's side of the family to emigrate from the village of Louboulou to Pointe-Noire. It was because of him we had all come to live in Pointe-Noire, with the exception of my mother, who made her own way here, to try to forget my natural father. Uncle Albert had come first, and once he'd set himself up he sent for his younger brother, Uncle René. After that his younger sisters arrived – my mother's older sisters – Aunt Dorothée and Aunt Sabine. When my mother arrived she brought with her the youngest of all the brothers and sisters, Uncle Mompéro. And as my maternal grandfather Grégoire Moukila was polygamous – twelve wives and more than fifty children – Uncle Albert gradually assembled them all at the rue de Louboulu, as his own professional position became more secure. Another of my uncles, who I was very close to, arrived by this route, Jean-Pierre Matété, who had the same father as my mother. With so many members of the family living in this street, Uncle Albert got the authorities to agree to change the name to rue de Louboulu, in honour of this small corner of the Bouenza district, of which our grandfather, Grégoire Moukila, became chief in the mid-1900s. In a way the street was like our own village. Most of the houses had been built by people from our district, though in later years some of them had sold their homes, gradually allowing people we didn't know to move in. Because my uncle worked in electricity everyone got free power. A wire simply had to be passed from one household through to the next, and suddenly we went from storm lantern to light bulb, from coal iron to electric iron.

The city council agreed to Uncle Albert's request, after he'd paid backhanders to a few of the government employees who then came and raised their glasses, shamelessly, at the renaming ceremony for the street. Every week members of the family would drop in to see Uncle Albert, and when he withdrew into his bedroom you knew he would re-emerge with some money to give the visitor. Broadly speaking, though it was not to be said out loud, you went round to Uncle Albert's in the hope of leaving again with a few thousand CFA francs. If people arrived while he was having his siesta they would hang around in the yard, pretending to chat with Gilbert and Bienvenüe, my uncle's twins, my cousins, with whom I spent much of my childhood. The twins understood what was going on, and sensed that their father was basically the family bank. Sometimes, so he wouldn't be disturbed while he was resting, Uncle Albert would place a packet of banknotes on the table and leave it to his wife, Ma Ngudi, to distribute them to the various visitors.

My mother would also stop off at the rue de Louboulu. Not to pick up money, but to hand some over to Ma Ngudi, because I sometimes lived at my uncle's for a while. Maman Pauline had requested this, 'in the interests of Albert's nephew'. Ma Ngudi was said to be good with children who didn't eat enough – sometimes I would eat only the meat, and leave the fufu and manioc.

One evening my mother came to pick me up at Uncle Albert's, and Marcel, my father's bête noire, just happened to be hanging around close by. By pure coincidence, Papa Roger, on his way back from work, had also decided to thank my uncle and his wife for having me to stay with them, and probably to leave a little envelope for my cousins Bienvenüe and Gilbert, as he often did.

My mother and I were still saying goodbye to Uncle Albert when we heard a great rumpus out in the street. It had to be a fight, because all the kids in the neighbourhood were shouting:

'Ali boma yé! Ali boma yé! Ali boma yé!'

It was the famous cry of the Zaireans at the 'May 20th' Stadium during the legendary fight between Muhammad Ali and George Foreman. In both Congos, it had become customary to chant it at any brawl.

We all dashed outside into the street, and found a real punch-up going on, which had brought the entire Rex neighbourhood running to the rue du Louboulou. Marcel and my father were on the ground, covered in dust, and Papa Roger was on top, despite being so much smaller than the other guy, who seemed to me to be some kind of colossus, measuring nearly two metres, a good head taller than most houses in the street. Each time Marcel tried to get to his feet and catch my father off guard, the local people, including several members of our family, caught hold of his shirt or one of his feet, and he lost his balance again, to Papa Roger's advantage. Picking a fight in the middle of this group, where we were as good as joined at the hip, was equivalent to signing his own death warrant.

My mother yelled at the top of her voice:

'Roger! Leave the guy alone! He hasn't done anything!'

My father wouldn't let go of Marcel's neck.

'I'll kill him! I'll kill him!'

Buoyed up by the excitement of the group, he was leaping around, striking karate poses which he'd seen in the film *The Wrecking Crew*, butting him, kicking him, kneeing him, and again, till Marcel, his face all bloodied, managed to work himself free and make a run for it. The whole neighbourhood ran after him. Everyone had a piece of wood or a stone in their hands.

'They'll kill him!' shrieked my mother.

'We sure will!' came a voice from the crowd.

You couldn't tell who was throwing the stones and who the bits of wood, which Marcel was just managing to dodge. He had long legs and ran as though death itself was at his heels. In a few strides he crossed the Avenue of Independence and vanished into thin air in the winding streets of the Trois-Cents neighbourhood, the haunt of the prostitutes from Zaire. His pursuers knew not to go looking for him on that territory, where a fight could quickly turn into a general riot.

Back at our house, my parents were rowing fiercely. My mother was telling my father it was a coincidence that Marcel happened to be in the rue de Louboulou. My father didn't believe her, and was convinced that Maman Pauline had arranged a meeting with him, and that Uncle Albert was in on it, as were the entire Bembé tribe in the rue de Louboulou.

'So then why did the very people from my tribe that you're accusing take your side?'

My father didn't answer that. Proof, perhaps, that he realised my maternal family had been rooting for him, and he'd been carried away by suspicion and rage…

My mother is a miss

The photo's in black and white, with a bit torn off at
the bottom, on the right-hand side. It was taken
at the end of the 1970s, one afternoon in the Joli-Soir district.
I had come to meet my parents in this bar, where we are all
sitting at a table. The two of them have glasses raised to their
lips, and mine is on the table. It's filled with beer, my mother
insisted on this, she didn't want anyone to think I was only
there for the photo. We had to make it look like I had been
sitting drinking with them for some time. I can still hear my
mother acting like some finicky film director, to the photographer's slight surprise:

'Hold on, monsieur, we're not ready! First get rid of those
flies buzzing round the table! A fine way to mess up people's
photos! I'll tell you when to press the button!'

She swept her eyes across the room, hoping she could put off
the moment when he took the picture. A few people entered and
were making their way to the back of the bar. She grabbed her
chance:

'What's all this, then? Did you see that? You can't even take
a photo in this country these days, not since President Marien
Ngouabi died! Tell them to stop coming in for a moment!'

Then, turning her attention to us:

'And you two, act as though the photographer wasn't there!

Especially you, Roger, whenever someone takes your photo you look all tensed up like a snail that doesn't know which way to turn! What way is that to behave? And you, boy, sit properly now. Sit up straight like a boy scout, like a boy who's proud to be sitting there between his papa and mama!'

Despite all these precautions, at which the photographer's annoyance grew, she failed to notice a fourth glass on the table, to my left, in front of Papa Roger. He had bought a drink for the photographer, who had knocked it back in one, without saying thank you, eager to get on with the serious business. Instead of moving his glass out of the way, he had left it there. He seemed completely overwhelmed by his job, which, in order for him to make any money at all, required him to go all round town, from one bar to another, persuading people to have their photos taken. He wrote down your address in an old notebook and came round to your house the next day with the picture. You had to pay him a deposit beforehand. He made sure to print several copies of the same image, since if it turned out to be a masterpiece, everyone was going to want one. He was known in most districts of Pointe-Noire by now. And that day he was blowing his own trumpet in front of my parents, saying:

'I'm the only one in this town with a Hasselblad SWC! Even the Americans used one when they went up into space! Do the other photographers in this town have one? No they do not! Just me! That's why they call me Mr Hasselblad SWC!'

Could anyone verify his claims? No one understood his gibberish anyway, all you saw was him pressing a button, and a flash that went off just like on any other camera. But my mother cut him short:

'Stop prattling and tell us how much the photo costs!'

Mr Hasselblad SWC struck up a ridiculous pose with his camera and, in the blink of an eye, the flash exploded in our faces…

The photo looks different to me now. Perhaps because I'm looking at it in the town where it was taken. It's as though in Europe or in America it keeps its secrets hidden. I look more closely. My mother dominates the picture. All you see, practically, is her and the scarf round her head. She seems more relaxed than my father and I, who are both trying to squeeze into the small amount of space she's left us. She wanted to be the one people saw when they looked at the photo. We were just there to highlight her presence, the principal's impact being very much dependent on the involvement of those playing the secondary roles. This was clearly the impression she wished to create, with the way she is leaning slightly to the right, as though my father and I no longer existed, or as though we were intruding on what she considered her moment of glory, which she would leave for posterity.

She is looking at the camera lens with a little smile, showing she has found the perfect pose. She doesn't know I've got my mouth open, a blank expression, big wide eyes that seem to be asking what the point of this photo is. Normally she would have reminded me:

'Sit up straight, look, we're having our picture taken!'

She'd have told me to close my mouth, she didn't like this expression, considering it unworthy and unflattering.

My shirt is hanging open – perhaps I had lost my buttons again, 'like an idiot', as my mother would have said. I admit that buttoning up my shirt was not a priority. I often had my shirt with all the buttons in the wrong holes.

Now I notice various details that I haven't seen before. For example, my mother's right shoulder seems to be crushing me, while my father's trying to keep us propped up. That's why his head is pressed up against mine. I can see, too, my father's fingers on my mother's left shoulder. I think it must be his left arm holding us up and without it we wouldn't have managed to hold the pose. Lastly, the marks left by the bottles on the surface of the table suggest the waiters didn't wipe them very often…

Two women

I called her 'Grandma Hélène', but she was really my aunt, and she lived in the rue de Louboulou, just behind Uncle Albert's house. She went everywhere barefoot, and stopped outside every house to offer vegetables, fruit, manioc, foufou or a demijohn of palm wine. Grandma Hélène was one of those people who you think has to have been born old, toothless, white haired, hesitant in her movements, like a stray gastropod, it was so impossible to imagine her young. You couldn't tell her age, she didn't know herself, having lived her entire life without an identity card or a birth certificate. In her day, to obtain such documents, you had to pay a visit to the colonial authorities, who measured your height, inspected the state of your teeth and made a guess at an approximate year of birth with the famous expression: 'Born around....'. Neither her husband, Old Joseph, nor she herself ever bothered to do this, particularly since several of the traditional chiefs, whose opposition to the colonial administration took particularly imaginative forms, spread rumours to the effect that the whites had a secret plan: anyone who agreed to have civil papers drawn up for them would have their souls carried off to Europe. These individuals would once again become slaves, and would undergo the fateful 'voyage' of the slave trade, which would take them, via Europe, all the way to America, where they would be sold to

the highest bidder and set to work from dawn to dusk in plantations owned by their brutal masters. According to these highly
placed sources, this was how the whites had created the slave
trade, knowing they would never have the physical strength to
confront the blacks and take them captive. Fear ruled, like the
fear that gripped the villagers when the first cameras arrived in
their land. At the time every possible argument – most of them
outlandish in the extreme – was used to dissuade people from
allowing themselves to be photographed. Just look at Europe,
which only managed to keep going by hijacking souls and
spirits. They spoke admiringly of their ancestors, who, when
photographed against their wishes, simply didn't appear on the
image, because they were more mystical than the white man,
and had taken the precaution of covering their souls with a kind
of anti-flash cover.

In any case, no one would have asked Grandma Hélène or
her husband their age, it would have implied they were too old
and should be thinking about moving on to that distant country
where, the Bembé believe, the sun never rises. Old Joseph
looked so strong, people always thought he must be several years
younger than his wife. A man of few words, he would sit out in
the sun – source of all longevity, he believed – and thoughtfully watch time passing, just sitting on his own front doorstep.
His left eye was useless, the entire surface of the pupil covered
over by a large, pale tumour. He could now see only through
the other eye, but even so, not one detail of the comings and
goings in his yard escaped him. Some were afraid of his sickly
eye, rambling on about the old man using it in the dark to find
out the sorcerers' tricks and foil them, before it was too late.

Their firstborn daughter, Mâ Germaine, seemed as old as
them. There was a rumour that the couple had handed down

the secret of long life to their descendants. Grandma Hélène was aware of this, and would babble crossly:

'We're already old, age has forgotten us, and we've forgotten it too. That's the secret of our longevity...'

Old Joseph was rather overshadowed by Grandma Hélène, but she herself led a busy life, to say the least, continually checking that no one she knew wore a mask of despair. If they did, she would go over to them, lift it off, and mumble some comforting words, assuring them things would be much better tomorrow. She'd been nicknamed 'Mother Teresa' because though she had more than ten children under her roof she put the interests of others even before those of her own offspring. Idle gossips were quick to imply that each time you got a gift from Grandma Hélène she took a year off your life to extend her own and that of her husband and children. Hence the uncouth manner in which some people rejected the old lady's generosity, accusing her of being a witch.

In actual fact, in all the time since she arrived from Louboulou she had never grown used to the idea that everything here was different, and that life in the city was unlike life back in the village in every way. Here an act of kindness drew suspicion. There it was a sacred duty, designed to keep the ungrateful, the selfish and individualists away from the village. In her mind, Pointe-Noire, and in particular the rue de Louboulou, was her village, it had simply been relocated, and because of this she had an obligation, as a peasant woman in possession of vast plantations in her home country, to share what she possessed with the population, whoever they were, that was the way she had been brought up.

She was so highly respected, she had become like a patriarch of the tribe, a kind of protective presence, even, watching over our family and the inhabitants of the rue de Louboulou. She would prepare food in a huge aluminium pot, then turn up in the street, grab hold of any child who happened to be passing, and sit them down in front of a large, steaming portion. Gluttons were only too delighted, along with various parasites and outright crooks, who knew you only had to drift past her house at mealtimes to get yourself a square meal. Which is probably why several adults could be found pacing up and down her yard, emerging fit to burst, like boa constrictors who've swallowed an antelope. We children, on the other hand, didn't hang around her that much; to us her generosity felt like a punishment in disguise, particularly as once we had finished eating Grandma Hélène would applaud, then say, with a great big smile:

'Well done, children! Well done! And now give me a belch, to show how good it was! Come on, a nice big belch! Quick!'

This was another of the customs she had brought with her from the village: she needed to hear her guest belch, or her face would grow troubled, and she felt her food could not have been nice. But even after you belched – to her delight – she would pile up your plate again and stand in front of you, to make sure you finished it, and gave another belch, even louder than the last. And she would point out which bit of meat to eat first, even instructing you to drink lots, to make sure your food 'went down well' and you had enough room in your stomach for even more. Even while one cooking pot emptied, as she served up food to all comers, she was getting the next one on the fire, and reeling off from memory the names of people who hadn't eaten, with a large wooden spoon in her hands:

'I know Albert's twins, Gilbert and Bienvenüe, haven't come by yet, or Jean-Pierre Matété and Mompéro, who were supposed to drop in today. And then there's Sabine and Dorothée, and I mustn't forget Kengué, Kimangou, Mizélé, Ndomba, Ndongui, Miyalou Kihouari, Milébé, Matété, Nkouaka, Marie, Véronique, Poupy, Firmin, Abeille, Jean de Dieu or René...'

You'd hear her saying to herself as she roamed round her kitchen in a cloud of smoke:

'I'm worried I'll run out of manioc! Who else have I forgotten?'

One time, when we just weren't hungry, we thought we'd found a way of avoiding her. You just had to go via the street behind, parallel to the rue de Louboulou. It worked for a while, and Grandma Hélène got in a great state over the defection of so many kids:

'Where have all the children gone? Are their parents stopping them from coming to eat here? I've been keeping their food for two days now, I'm sick of heating it up!'

It was upsetting to see her go to a public tip three days later and unload the rotting food, with tears in her eyes, while emaciated stray dogs circled around. She cursed herself for having such an ungrateful family, but the next day she'd start over again, doing what she did best in this world: cooking for others.

Dieudonné Ngoulou, a hearty eater, who had remained loyal to her, and who we were mean to, because he was the weakest and most cowardly of all of us, revealed all to the old lady. Imagine our surprise when we found Grandma Hélène watching out for us at the corner of the rue de Louboulou and the Avenue of Independence at mealtimes, crouching down behind a mango tree, still with her legendary wooden spoon in her hands. Like a wounded cat fighting back, she would leap out, catch the crafty beggar by his shirt and drag him bodily back to her kitchen:

'Thought you could pull a fast one on me, did you? Thought

you were cleverer than me? Well, you can eat three helpings for me today, because I haven't seen you for three days! You need to catch up! Come on, hurry up, I've no time to waste!'

She had an obsessive fear of whites, mixed with absolute deference. She firmly believed that a few days before her death, a white woman would come and kiss her on the forehead, and open the doors to the next world, so she could pass on and complete up there what she had begun here below.

'It's the whites who take people off to the country where the sun never rises, and I know a white woman will come to fetch me when my time comes…'

She would say this whenever there was a wake in the neighbourhood. Most people dismissed it as the ramblings of an elderly person whose mental faculties were waning as she approached the fateful day of her demise. But Grandma Hélène took it seriously.

Several months before developing the illness which would paralyse her, she began putting her affairs in order, to people's surprise:

'My body's packing up. I'm getting sicker all the time. I can't cook properly any more. The white woman's not far off now, I see her in my dreams. I wish she'd hurry up and set me free…'

She bought a large metal trunk and a suitcase, and put them in a corner of the dining room, under an old piece of furniture. Her things were inside, and she could be heard muttering:

'I'll be cooking for other people in the land where the sun never rises, so I mustn't forget my spoon… I don't care about pots, they've got them up there, but I'm not going without my wooden spoon, it's what gives my food its flavour…'

Sometimes she would get up in the night to check everything was in order, that she hadn't forgotten anything. Reassured, after a session of careful stocktaking, which sounded like a litany of her final wishes, she would go back to bed, lie down, fold her arms and, finally, close her eyes. All this time, the illness was gnawing away at her puny, pain-racked body.

Everyone knew that the fateful hour could not be long now, as for several months she had cooked for no one and had lain pinned to her mattress in the dining room, her eyes riveted on her bags, and on the photo of the Virgin Mary. When they told her I was coming any day now, she didn't react and her visitors thought she must have forgotten who I was…

At the entrance to Grandma Hélène's plot, stifling her emotion at seeing me after all these years, Mâ Germaine warns me:

'She won't recognise you. She doesn't even know I'm her daughter now, and every time I go near her she's terrified, as though I'm an evil spirit! Since she took to her bed, she hasn't known anyone. And she hasn't seen you for twenty-three years…'

I go on into the room anyway. The first thing I see are the old lady's belongings, piled up in a corner. The Virgin Mary looks sad, hanging there on the wall. It smells like a stable, and no one thinks to open a window to air it.

I go over to the mosquito net and see a human shape inside it, twitching from time to time. It's her, the old lady. Covered in white sheets of doubtful cleanliness, she lies still now, prisoner of a mysterious illness, which forces her to stay stretched out on her back, excreting and pissing on to the mattress, which is on the floor. She sees the visitors at a distance and groans:

'I'm in pain, I'm in terrible pain…'

Grandma Hélène is by now a human wreck, bound to this

world only by the air she breathes. Curled up inside her white mosquito net, as though she's already in a coffin, she looks almost like a corpse awaiting burial…

'She won't recognise you,' insists Mâ Germaine.

I ignore her warning and draw aside the mosquito net, so I can see her.

There she is, curled up in the foetal position, her face relaxed. She senses my presence and opens her eyes as I lean over towards her.

With a quick movement, she grasps hold of my hand:

'Is that you?'

Though I am not sure whether she has really recognised me, I nod. And then, to my utter amazement, I hear her babbling:

'You see, my child, I'm proud of myself now, the food I gave you when you were a child has made you grow up big and strong, you're nearly two metres tall… But anyway, that's all in the past now, it's done with, and I'm dying now, like your mother, Pauline Kengué, and your father, Kimongou Roger, and your aunts, Bouanga Sabine and Dorothée Louhounou, and your uncles, Albert Moukila and René Mabanckou, except at least I've been lucky enough to see you before I go to join them…'

'You aren't going to die, Grandma…'

'Oh, look at me, what have I become? A corpse! Was I like this when you left me? It upsets people to see me like this… If I still had the strength I would have killed myself, but I can't move without help now, and no one wants to help me leave this life, not even my husband…'

She begins to shudder, there is fear in her eyes:

'There she is! There she is! Help me chase her away!'

'Chase who away, Grandma? What?'

'The shadow behind you!'

'That's not a shadow, Grandma, it's someone who's come with me and...'

'It's a shadow, I'm telling you, I see them all the time now! The Virgin Mary helps me chase them away. Please, help me chase that shadow there, watching me... Just do it for me.'

'Grandma, that's my girlfriend, we arrived together from France a few days ago and...'

'Is she black or is she white?'

'She's white.'

'Are you sure?'

'Yes.'

'Oh, then I'm saved! I've waited for her for years. I can go now, she's come to set me free...'

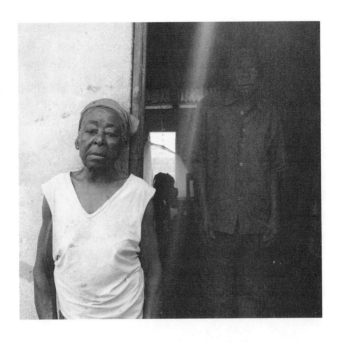

My mother's castle

At the family reunion to celebrate my arrival, I noticed two empty chairs opposite me, and two glasses filled with palm wine placed before each of them. Everyone had an explanation, except me. Just to be clear, I asked whether we were waiting for two more people, because there were already over thirty of us on the plot left by my mother. Looking embarrassed, a cousin whispered in my ear:

'It's your mother and father sitting on the two chairs. You think they are empty but in fact they are taken…'

And she explained that other members of the family were absent, at rest in the Mont-Kamba cemetery, the burial place for the common people, at the other end of town…

I walked round 'Maman Pauline's plot', as they say here. There is a tiny hut tucked away in one corner of the property. Almost a blemish on this neighbourhood of solid buildings, with electricity. Every property in the Voungou neighbourhood has been carefully fenced in. Except ours, where the hut seems to have pointedly refused this practice, preferring the mode of the old communist regime, where we were told that everything belonged to 'the people, and the people alone'. There was no point marking out the limits of your land, because no one, in principle, owned anything, only the state, which could exercise its own prerogative and dispossess inhabitants in the 'collective interest'.

Once the traditional chiefs started to sell off land, it was sensible to build 'something' on the land you acquired, in case those no-good dealers from the city sold it with false property deeds. These kinds of makeshift dwellings were known as 'houses for now', since the inhabitants hoped to put up comfortable homes at some point in the future. They usually died without having built the house of their dreams, having never had the means to do so.

My mother acquired her plot in February 1979. I had just turned thirteen and was at Trois Glorieueses secondary school. I can still remember the seller coming round, a chief of the Vili people, who bargained with my mother and tried to increase her bid, claiming he had other, higher offers. My mother, an experienced businesswoman, pretended to have lost interest in the purchase and indicated to the seller that he could do a deal with the highest bidder, since she had now found another piece of land, in a better position, in the centre of town.

A week later, the seller came back to see us in the studio we rented in the Fonds Tié-Tié neighbourhood. He had changed his tune, and modified his exorbitant demands. Where had all those clients gone, who'd been fighting to get in the door? He breathed not one word about them. The moment he accepted my mother's offer of a beer, I knew he had capitulated, and had fallen into the trap skilfully laid for him by Maman Pauline, on whose lips I detected a look of triumph. She even rejected the average selling price for the neighbourhood.

'I'm not buying this land for myself, it's for my son,' I heard her argue.

I don't know what other arguments she put forward, but I saw her take out some crumpled notes, unfold each one, and count out loud under the watchful eye of the greedy vendor. The trader stuffed the money into a plastic bag which he pulled out of the back pocket of his trousers. Which convinced me that the sale would definitely be completed that day, since he had thought to bring along something to put the money in.

They arranged a rendezvous for the following day, to finalise the sale with the authorities.

We had become house owners, and my father was not to learn of it until later, on the day we moved in...

We planted maize on the land we had just acquired. But that wasn't enough, we needed to give a clear sign to the crooks that we were the new owners. Uncle Mompéro, my mother's younger brother, set about building a house made of wooden planks. I stood behind him, and from time to time he asked me to hand him the saw, the set square, the nails or the boards. I was proud to feel useful, to feel that I too, with my little hands, was contributing to the construction of our home. While the building work was going on, my mother prepared food in a corner, which we would eat during the afternoon break. She had engaged two Zairean builders, because she wanted a proper floor, even if the house had to be of planks. In less than a week, the house had taken shape, standing in the field of maize. We had left the house we were renting in the Fonds Tié-Tié neighbourhood and had moved in one morning, even though a storm was looming, threatening a heavy downpour. Our house had two tiny bedrooms and a small living room. I had one room, my parents the other. Uncle Mompéro himself slept in the living room in a bed he had built himself. And when two members of the family arrived from their villages – my mother's cousin, Grand Poupy, and Papa Roger's niece, Ya Nsoni – I let the latter have my room and slept in the living room with my uncle, together in the same bed. Every evening Grand Poupy spread a mat on the ground, and some nights I slept with him.

Back here again, I find it hard to believe this is the same house we had then. The family reunion is being held in the middle of the yard. My facial expression, one of utter astonishment, is being closely watched.

Uncle Mompéro, who took me on a tour of the plot as soon as I arrived, revealed that a part of the house had been 'cut off', leaving only the one room, where he sleeps.

'Can we go in and look?' I asked.

'No, I don't want you to go inside...'

I didn't insist, and we went back into the yard, where things were beginning to liven up since the drinks had arrived...

Towards the end of the party, I leaned over to my cousin Kihouari, to ask him for the 'right to occupy' paper that my mother signed back then. It is a pink piece of paper handed out by the land registry office, bearing the family name and forename of my mother. It says that the land has a surface area of four hundred square metres. Just looking at it, I doubt it is as big as that. Kihouari tells me that there are indeed four hundred metres, as stated in the description from the land registry, but our neighbours at the back encroached by several square metres when they built the wall dividing our land from theirs.

'This wall is actually on our land...' he concluded, looking resigned.

I recall that in the past the two plots were separated only by some stakes and barbed wire. At that time our neighbours had also built a 'house for now', a bit bigger than ours. Now they have a huge, permanent structure and this wall, which stops us seeing what's going on at their place.

Uncle Mompéro is listening in and gathers what Kihouari is telling me. My uncle adds, in quite a loud voice, as though he wants the whole family to hear:

'After we buried my sister, Pauline Kengué, the neighbours didn't wait even two weeks, they put up this ridiculous wall without even asking us! And they pinched a few square metres from us while they were about it! Is that acceptable, d'you think? That wall is on our land!'

There was a general murmur of discontent. Everyone wants to express their exasperation in the face of this injustice. They wait for my reaction.

I reassure them:

'Tomorrow I'll go to the land registry office and ask them to come and remeasure the dimensions of this plot. We can't let them get away with it, it's robbery!'

A storm of applause greets my remarks. Only Kihouari doesn't join in, surprisingly, since I was sure he would be in favour of my plan.

He gives me a nod and we move away from the group to a corner of the plot, just behind the hut. His face is very serious now. He puts his hand on my left shoulder.

'*Please* don't do what you're planning tomorrow…'

'What do you mean?'

'Don't go to the land registry office…'

'Are you kidding? They're stealing square metres from us, and you want to let it go? Tell me the truth now: have the neighbours been slipping you money?'

'No, absolutely not! How can you think such a thing! Would I, Kihouari, sell off part of my own aunt's land?'

'Well, what's the problem, then?'

He's silent for a moment, looking over at the rest of the family. The group is getting gradually smaller. Some people are starting to leave, others are watching us, wondering what we are cooking up, over by the old shack.

Kihouari clears his throat:

'I think I had better tell you something very important, you seem out of touch with reality since you moved away...'

I had never seen him look so serious. The death of his mother, Dorothée Lohounou – another of my mother's older sisters – must have brought him face to face with his responsibilities: as the oldest of a dozen or more sisters and brothers, he had had to become wise before his time.

'These neighbours you want to go for, they're a bit like our family too. The owner, Monsieur Goma, died one year after Aunt Pauline Kengué. Monsieur Goma's wife got kicked out like a sick dog by the brothers of the deceased. As for the children, they are scattered in their mother's village. Two of them, Anicet and Apollo, live in France and London, and no one ever hears from them. They must be about your age, you used to play together in our yard and theirs. You even used to eat at their house, and sometimes they came and ate at ours. Now the younger brother of the late Monsieur Goma looks after their plot. He's a bit strange, it's true, but even so, it's thanks to him that the plot hasn't been sold by the same people who threw out the widow and wanted to get their hands on the inheritance and disinherit the children! I respect him for that if for nothing else. Did you notice he dropped by to say hello and insisted on appearing in the photos we took when you arrived? His name is Mesmin, he knew you when you were a boy, that was his way of showing you he was practically a member of the family. So what would be the good at this stage of having a confrontation before the tribunal? You're going to go back to Europe, or America, and you'll leave us with hot potatoes in our hands. When we leave this life we leave whatever we owned on earth, why get into a fight over it now...?'

I am speechless. Kihouari goes back to join the family, and I stand there staring at the little hut.

I walk around the shack and trip over some stones propped up against the main façade. They used to be the two entrance steps. The seasons have worn them away, leaving just this scattered debris, which no one dares move, out of respect for my mother's memory. The old slats of wood, bound by a kind of unshakeable solidarity, hold together, defying time. On the left, by the only window, I notice some bits of wood and plank that must have broken off with wear and tear. It wouldn't occur to anyone to make a fire with them, they're used to prop up the corners, to stop the shack falling down for as long as possible. Strings and pieces of wood positioned on the sheet metal keep the roof in place. The main door has been eaten away at the bottom by termites.

Yes, I used to sleep there. My dreams were less confined than the space we lived in. At least when I closed my eyes and sleep lent me wings to fly, I found myself in a vast kingdom, not in a shack that looks today like a fisherman's hut straight out of *The Old Man and the Sea*, or even *The Old Man Who Read Love Stories*.

I've been so concerned with the shack, I've overlooked a solidly built structure on the plot, with three little studios attached. Two are occupied by tenants, and the third by Kihouari's little brother, his wife and three children.

Kihouari comes up behind me:

'Aunt Pauline Kengué began the work on the solid structure… At the time she died there were only the two studios, we added the third…'

The day is almost over. A taxi draws up outside the plot. Uncle Jean-Pierre Matété called for it. I'm just about to climb in, when I feel once more the presence of Kihouari at my back.

'Brother, the old shack is a disgrace to the family, we're going to pull it down and put something else in its place...'

I give him a furious look.

'No way! I'm going to restore it, the place is meaningless without the shack...'

Before getting into the car I add:

'It's my mother's castle...'

He looks at me pityingly, unable to understand why I should be more interested in the hut than in the solid structure, of which he is visibly proud. He's almost disappointed in me when I conclude:

'The one I'm going to pull down is the solid building, I'll replace it with another one... I will start work next year.'

The taxi sets off, and Uncle Mompéro, Uncle Matété and Grand Poupy wave goodbye from a distance. I'll be back one day...

A fistful of dollars

I'm wandering through the Voungou neighbourhood in the late afternoon. Maybe in search of clues to remind me of my childhood games. Occasionally I stand still for a few seconds and close my eyes, sure I don't need them to see the true face of the things jostling about in my mind, their contours blurred with time. Passers-by can sense I'm not local – or am no longer. Who, besides the town madmen, would dare stand around, for example, gazing at a pile of rubbish, or the carcass of an animal, getting emotional over the clucking of a hen, perched, inexplicably, on a table in the empty market?

The family members I saw yesterday at our reunion don't know that I am only two hundred metres from my mother's property, like a criminal returning to the place of the crime to reassure himself that he made no mistakes, or to erase any clues that might lead the investigators to his door. If they saw me, they would improvise another party, with empty chairs in memory of my parents.

So I take the small backstreets, with my cap jammed right down to the top of my eyebrows. Just as I reach an intersection and let two taxis go by before crossing the marketplace, I hear a female voice call me from somewhere ahead:

'Little brother! Hey, little brother!'

I look up, and try to hide my surprise: it's Georgette.

She's standing at a pavement table outside a small bar. She is number two of the eight children my father had with my 'second mother', Maman Martine. I can see Yaya Gaston behind her, too, sitting at a table with a bottle of Pelforth. He's wearing sunglasses and the orange overalls you see on the men who work in the warehouses down at the seaport of Pointe-Noire. His is scruffy, stained with black grease marks. It looks like he never takes it off, and wears the same outfit for work and around town. He waves me over to join them.

It seems strange to bump into them by chance, and I think to myself that such coincidences only happen in spaghetti westerns, where the protagonists pop up out of nowhere, exchange a few angry words, draw their guns and shoot at each other. What are they doing in this place, overlooking my late mother's property?

'Come on, come and have a drink with us,' insists Georgette, though showing no particular pleasure at seeing me after all these years.

Hesitantly, I enter the bar.

Georgette, who is now over fifty, refusing to accept the evidence of her years, whitens her skin and dyes her hair. Even so, you can see grey hairs on her temples and at the nape of her neck. She's a tiny thing, with Papa Roger's features – we always called her 'Photocopy', even though she hated it. Yaya Gaston seems to have come to terms with the passage of time, though he certainly looks his age, and more. His lips are stained red with drink, and he has a badly trimmed little beard. He tries to get up and hug me, but can't manage it.

'Don't get up!' Georgette says to him, trying to conceal from me what is blatantly obvious: our older brother is wasted, today and every day.

She points to a stool for me, and orders a beer. Stony faced, as though some unspoken resentment burns within her, she begins:

'So what are you doing here? D'you think we still need you?'

I take the knock without flinching. She lashes out again:

'You've been in Pointe-Noire for a few days now, and you haven't been to see us!'

Yaya Gaston interrupts his sister, and comes to my rescue:

'I saw you yesterday at your talk at the French Institute!'

Yes, I had seen him the previous day. My memory of our meeting was not a pleasant one. I had been upset on his behalf, but also for the memory of our father. I noticed his presence just as he was about to be ejected from the room for having disturbed the audience. Almost too drunk to stand, he kept asking for the microphone at the end of the talk, with the crowd jeering and laughing all around him. It was offered to him, he seized hold of it, but went on repeating over and over, 'Hello, hello, hello!', as though he was holding a telephone. Eventually he managed to say, to the great amusement of the three hundred people present:

'Hello, hello, hello! My name is Gaston. I am the great Yaya Gaston in the novel *Tomorrow I'll Be Twenty*, which talks about our late father, Papa Roger! I am the big brother of this gentleman here, the writer! We have the same father, he and I, same mother, same womb!'

A great commotion ran through the audience. Yaya Gaston, who had had the microphone snatched from him, found himself assailed with insults from all over the room. Seeing that the security guards were getting ready to evict him by force, I returned to my microphone and said:

'Let him be, he's my big brother…'

A deathly hush swept through the room, interrupted a few seconds later by Yaya Gaston's whoops of victory as he shouted over and over:

'What did I tell you? Did you hear what he said? He admits it, I'm his big brother, same father, same mother, same womb! Show some respect! Show some respect, you guys! I'm a person in a novel! I'm famous, people will talk about me even when I'm dead! How many of you can say you're people in a novel, eh? Zero! I'm telling you: same father, same mother, same womb! Go on, little brother, you finish your talk, I'll shut up now, I'll wait for you!'

Afterwards I'd had no choice but to arrange to meet him at my father's house in the next few days.

'Give me some money to get home!'

He pocketed the ten thousand CFA franc note I offered him and turned on his heels, muttering:

'We'll wait for you at the house! Maman Martine doesn't live in Pointe-Noire now, she went back to the village when Papa Roger died, but I'll send her the money you've brought for her. I'm going to tell everyone you're here…'

The night of the incident at the French Institute, I couldn't sleep. I counted the insects crashing into the light bulb over my head. Why did my brother feel the need to bring up our connection, and expose himself to humiliation before the audience which clearly included people who knew perfectly well that I had no brother or sister who were 'same father, same mother, same womb'? Did he really think that it was just blood that brings people together, not shared life experience? In any case, he was convinced that by affirming that we were brothers he would raise his esteem with the audience. On the other hand, if he had announced that I had been adopted by his father, he'd have looked like the worker in the vineyard who turns up at the twenty-fifth hour. I had been disturbed to see Yaya Gaston in such a state that evening. All that jeering had upset me; I felt as much the victim of it as he was himself. The public realised when they heard the catch in my voice, and saw I wasn't responding with the energy I'd had at the beginning of the talk. Yaya Gaston plays a significant part in my life, which is why he is one of the principal characters in *Tomorrow I'll Be Twenty*, where I portray him as someone who is obsessively clean, an idol, a hero, a real, proper big brother. He had taken me under his wing, and we slept in the same room at Papa Roger's house, despite the jealousy of his 'same father, same mother, same womb' brothers. Memories of that time still haunt me, especially Yaya Gaston's multiple girlfriends – including the generous Geneviève – who would take our little room by storm and were all madly in love with him.

I wanted to see my big brother again. I had done the right thing, I said to myself, in arranging to meet him in our father's house, because we wouldn't have been able to talk calmly with him in the excited state he'd been in that evening. But clearly he hadn't waited for the rendezvous and had been watching out for me together with Georgette, near my mother's house, from inside the bar, hoping they might see me.

I had never been very close to Georgette. She was always out with her friends, always running off somewhere, despite Papa Roger's fury. Constantly in conflict with Maman Martine, and sometimes with Yaya Gaston too, who we were meant to respect as the oldest of the family, Georgette had been a 'trendy' young woman. The way she dressed was on the verge of indecent, at a time when the young people of Pointe-Noire were attracted to the SAPE, the Society of Ambience-Makers and People of Elegance. Her lovers were 'Parisians', young men who came over from France to show off their over-the-top outfits during the dry season. Their skin had been whitened with products made from hydroquinone, and they had paunches – for them, a sign of elegance, since a rounded belly held up your belt and trousers more effectively than a flat one. The arrival of these young gods in Pointe-Noire stirred up trouble in families. The young girls lost their heads and turned rebellious, spending whole nights following the Parisians from bar to bar.

Seeing my sister again now, I realised at once that the ambush had been her idea, and that she had taken advantage of Yaya Gaston's drink problem. He was just going along with her.

The waiter places a beer in front of me.

'Drink it while it's cold,' advises Georgette, who seems to have calmed down a bit.

I do as she says, and she adds triumphantly:

'We knew you'd come and hang around your mother's plot, that's why we've been sitting here since late this morning! You always loved your mother more than your father!'

A young man of around thirty sits down at our table. Noticing my surprise, Georgette introduces him:

'This is Papa Roger's cousin, so he's your cousin too. I told him to come by. He'll take the money you could have given Papa Roger if he'd still been alive…'

Yaya Gaston nods his agreement:

'Don't worry, little brother, just give him fifty thousand CFA francs or a bit more and he'll be happy!'

Georgette leaps off her stool:

'What? Fifty thousand CFA francs? Gaston, do you know what you're saying? Is that kind of money going to bring Papa Roger back to us? What about me, then, how much would he give me? The same?'

Yaya Gaston says hastily:

'Calm down, sister, I'm sure our little brother won't give you less than a hundred thousand CFA francs! You know how generous he is!'

'No way! I won't be made fun of! I'm not accepting a little sum of money after he's been abroad all these years, never seeing us! Not once, since he left, did he ever send us a single money order! I need a million CFA francs! We buried our father, we spent money and he sent us nothing! Do you think I'll accept one hundred thousand CFA francs? Never! And if he gives me one hundred thousand CFA francs, I'll chuck them in the gutter, so there!'

I do a quick calculation: I've only got thirty thousand CFA francs in my pocket, far less than the staggering amount expected by my sister, whom I like less and less by the minute. I've stopped looking her in the eye; as far as I'm concerned she's a stranger to me now. All she talks about is money, not a word about the memory of our father. Basically, I'm supposed to reimburse the cost of Papa Roger's funeral. I wonder why my maternal family didn't take the same attitude, since I didn't attend Maman Pauline's funeral, and they never presented me with a bill. I try to control my irritation.

The so-called cousin of my father glances at my shoes from time to time. When he finally breaks his silence he says:

'Will you leave me those shoes?'

Yaya Gaston looks down at my Campers, really practical in this heat.

'Give me your shoes, little brother, not him. Papa's cousin can buy himself some with the money you give him…'

The so-called cousin looks at my jeans and white shirt. Before he even opens his mouth, Yaya Gaston gets in ahead of him:

'The shirt and jeans are taken! I'm having them. And my little brother can give me his suit as well, the one he was wearing at his talk…'

I can't think how to get out of this trap now. I need to find an excuse to leave.

I try asking:

'Are we still meeting at Papa's house?'

'Of course!' responds Georgette. 'We've told everyone, and they're all impatient for their share, but you have to give me mine now, because I don't want to get mixed up with the others when they all start fighting over it.'

'I haven't got anything on me, I didn't expect to find you here and…'

Yaya Gaston stops me: 'Listen, little brother, even if you only have twenty or thirty thousand CFA francs, give me that, for my fare. You can give us the rest when we have the reunion at the house.'

Georgette disagrees:

'Gaston, could you just shut up for once? Are you listening to what I'm saying? Are you looking for problems, or what?'

'He just needs to come an hour early, you go and sit in a bistro and he gives you the money!' suggests the 'cousin'.

Yaya Gaston backs him up. 'That's not a bad idea.'

Georgette's looking for a counter-argument, but she needs time. She decides to call a ceasefire.

'OK, we'll do that! For now just give us twenty or thirty thousand CFA francs for our transport.'

From where we are now, to my father's house, the cost of transport would be less than one thousand CFA francs. I'm tired of bargaining, and I dig into the pocket of my trousers. I manage to pull out a couple of notes and I put down twenty thousand CFA francs on the table. Georgette pockets them while the other two don't even blink. That leaves me with ten thousand CFA francs for my own fare home and a meal at Chez Gaspard.

As I get to my feet I know already that I won't be going to the family reunion, that I won't see Yaya Gaston again before I leave Pointe-Noire, because of Georgette.

I walk out of the bar while they're splitting up the twenty thousand CFA francs. They've already forgotten I exist, I can hear Georgette yelling at the other two:

'No! I'm taking twelve thousand, you two can split the other eight!'

Two-faced woman

My cousin Bienvenüe has been admitted to the Adolphe-Sicé hospital. Her twin brother Gilbert rang to tell me a few minutes ago.

'You're staying not far from the hospital, you could drop by and see her, she'd like that,' he insisted.

I don't think I will visit her, I won't have the courage, even though from the balcony of the apartment where I'm staying you can see the old colonial building, almost separate from the town, with its back to the Atlantic Ocean. Every morning since my arrival, I've stood here looking over at it, with a cup of coffee in my hand. When a crow settles on the roof, I think he must be adding up how many outings the ambulances make every day, between the city and this austere, crumbling place, often referred to by the locals as '*the death home*'. As a teenager, I passed by it on my way to the Karl Marx lycée, my stomach knotted with fear. I was convinced, like most of the students, that if you looked that way you'd bring bad luck on your family.

Grown-ups were quite clear that you must never 'show your face to the hospital', because it would take note of it, and remember it the day you passed through its doors and take your life. Some of us would cover our faces with our shirts as we came near the building. Others walked with their back to it. This fear was in fact fed by a character called Basile, who ran the hospital morgue. He was said to indulge in practices which were, to say the least, peculiar. He talked to corpses, and slapped them about if they wouldn't lie quietly in the cold rooms. He got particularly angry with the corpses of young girls he believed had led debauched lives. He slapped them, then made up their faces and piled them up like animals in a single coffin, while raging:

'Not so proud now, eh? Did you think you'd avoid the morgue? There's only one in this town! A human being's just a heap of flesh to me, flesh to feed the worms on!'

In the working-class districts, you'd pass Basile talking to invisible people, waving his arms around. Dogs ran after him, but never got too close to the little man with the angry face.

It was also widely known that Basile ate no meat, since he said he'd seen everything under the sun and to him there was no difference between cattle meat and human flesh…

Gilbert's voice was very faint:

'Bienvenüe is in Room One. You know, the room Papa was in…'

There was a silence, then he added, enigmatically:

'And since Papa died in that room…'

This conclusion rang like an acceptance of a fateful verdict, which he had been expecting. At a loss for words to reassure him, I simply asked:

'Isn't there any other room besides that one?'

'Everything's taken, Room One was only free because people would rather take the sick person home with them than keep them in there… But she was in pain, I couldn't do that…'

It's more than three decades, now, since Uncle Albert died after being admitted to hospital in Room One, where two other members of the family had been before him, Uncle Mouboungoulou and Uncle Makita, who both died 'after a long illness in Adolphe-Sicé hospital', as it said on the evening announcements on the radio, to avoid divulging the cause of death.

'Besides, there's no doctor qualified to treat her illness, I phoned Cousin Paulin, he's a doctor at the University Hospital in Brazzaville, he can't get to Pointe-Noire for three days. For now they're only giving Bienvenüe aspirin…'

'It'll be OK,' I murmured, 'don't forget she's your twin, the two of you are one body… If you believe your strength can pull her through, then it will.'

These words consoled my cousin, and as he hung up I heard him give a sigh of relief…

The day before she went into hospital, Bienvenüe was showing me another photo of when she was young. Deep down I knew she had only one thought in her mind: to throw off the thin body she had today, and catapult me back to the time when she was a beautiful young woman who turned the heads of the boys. She seemed to be apologising for what she had become. Which was not surprising, since it is common for sick people to take refuge in self-justification, whatever their state. Was there any particular reason she should act like this with me, who had known her when she was a beautiful young woman full of joy? Back then – she must have been around twelve – she, Gilbert and I all slept in the same bed. My presence between the twins evened things out in some way: I was a partition wall between them, a façade encouraging each of them to take their first steps towards independence, instead of seeing the world always from the point of view of their twinness. We made an inseparable trio, day and night. Gilbert, who was considered a bit of a spoiled child and an incurable egoist, nevertheless appreciated me sufficiently to lend me his favourite toys – in particular an electric train which, in our eyes, was the best toy on earth. You could travel the world with it, cross bridges, encounter Indian tribes, fight epic battles on the forecourts of deserted railway stations. Gilbert could also use me as a shield to hide his worst eccentricities. I remember, for instance, his fear of the dark. Uncle Albert often switched out the light to save energy, which did little to soothe my cousin's fears. He trembled in his bed, convinced that a monster with three heads, who, according to him, lived in the sewers of the rue du Louboulou, would come in the middle of the night and eat us all up. He described this creature using images taken from *Gidrah, the Three-headed Monster*, which his big brothers, Jean de Dieu, Firmin and Abeille, had shown on a projector in the yard, using a machine bought for them by their father. In this film, a prophetess from another planet comes down to earth to announce the imminent arrival of a three-headed dragon known as King Ghidorah. The only people who could possibly save us were Rodan and Godzilla, who had also returned, and would join forces with Mothra to defeat the terrifying creature. And since Gilbert was sure that Rodan and Godzilla wouldn't be turning up in the rue du Louboulou to offer their protection – because our street didn't feature on any map known to man – he asked to sleep in the middle, and would hide under the cover till first light. He was so frightened, he refused to use the little pot that was left out by my uncle at the entrance to the room for us to pee into. If he ventured out of his hiding place he might fall into the jaws of the three-headed monster. He sprayed the bed with quantities of hot urine and I got the blame in the morning, with no support from his sister, as Uncle Albert lectured me, and my own silence condemned me. In case I said anything, Gilbert would threaten to stop lending me his train, or still worse, to stop me sleeping with them...

Uncle Albert lavished every attention on the girl twin, setting her apart from the rest. This annoyed Gilbert, who would grumble in private, but calmed down once his sister handed over half the presents she had received from my uncle. My mother, too, had a special fondness for Bienvenüe. Whenever she visited Uncle Albert she would ask straight away:

'Where's my girl Bienvenüe?'

Bienvenüe would come out of her room and run to Maman Pauline, who would then ask Aunt Ma Ngudi if she could take her along with her to the Grand Marché for the day.

'But Pauline, Bienvenüe's your daughter! Why are you asking me permission to take her with you?'

Bienvenüe would come home in the evening with armloads of presents. I was secretly jealous of her, particularly since my mother had never taken me with her to the market, where I could have watched as she talked to customers while I nibbled a few peanuts, ate a ripe banana with Beninese doughnuts and drank ginger juice.

The fact was, we were scared of Bienvenüe, not because of her tempestuous, unpredictable character, but because of the belief in our tribe that a female twin was more powerful than the male. As such, the minute Bienvenüe got angry, we dashed off, till she came to find us, and reassured us:

'Come back, both of you, I won't put a curse on you, I'm not angry now...'

The reason Gilbert and I ran off to hide in Grandma Hélène's yard was because there was another belief that when a female twin got angry she could block up your ears for an hour or more.

So what about Gilbert? What powers did he have? No one knew, he had probably passed them to his sister as was said to happen between non-identical twins, opposition of the sexes always being, it was said, to the advantage of the girl.

Anyway, Bienvenüe was pleased to see me, and to show me her photos, but her brother had omitted to tell me that he would be taking her to the hospital the next day. While I was there he just stood by and watched his sister's display of euphoria as she wallowed in nostalgia, her eyes shining bright.

'What you been doing these twenty-three years abroad, then? I'd even forgotten you were a bit taller than Gilbert!'

As though she didn't believe the photos I had seen would be enough to remind me how beautiful she'd been, she asked her brother to go and take down from the wall another of her favourite photos.

'I want to be photographed with that photo!'

She sat down in the green armchair in the living room, with the photo placed in clear view on her knees, allowing herself to be photographed with the circumspect smile that convinced me she did still have sufficient energy to battle with the illness, which was getting worse by the day.

I looked her straight in the eyes:

'You're going to be OK, I promise you…'

She batted off the flies that had tried to settle on her swollen feet, and began to offer excuses:

'It's my blood… it's stopped circulating properly and my kidneys are a bit blocked… The flies like that…'

I looked up at the living room ceiling, showing the marks of rainwater, of imminent collapse, perhaps.

'I need to do some repairs,' Gilbert murmured, a little embarrassed by my inspection.

The light was beginning to fade. I kissed Bienvenüe and the children. Gilbert wanted to come with me as far as the Avenue of Independence, where I would pick up a taxi. Bienvenüe stood at the entrance to the plot with her daughter, her nephews, her nieces, and watched us grow smaller, and no doubt thought to herself that this was the last time we would see each other...

A crow has just come to settle on the roof of the hospital. I don't think it brings bad news. Because something tells me Bienvenüe will recover from her illness. And yet the bird is looking over this way and is spreading its wings, as though preparing to come over to me. The road past the Institut Français is empty of traffic now. I suddenly feel terribly anxious. I drink my coffee in one gulp, and come back into the living room, to read through the notes I've taken so far, and continue writing this book...

Children of paradise

I have a lot of 'nieces' and 'nephews' now. A small group gathers round me in Uncle Albert's yard, devouring me with their huge eyes, pulling at my shirt with their little hands. If I move, the whole buzzing little cluster follows me; I stop, and they stop too, afraid, I think, that I might disappear. For these kids I'm like an apparition, a shadow that will vanish with the setting sun. In their minds I'm just a character, artfully constructed by their parents, to the point where the poor kids actually think I can heal the lame and restore sight to the blind. One of them – the tallest – sniffs at me like a dog trying to identify his master after a long absence. They all want to be the first to speak. One wants sandals, and embarks on a series of elaborate explanations:

''Cause you know, Uncle, if you don't have new sandals, you can't get to school on time, you have to spend two hours in the street mending them and when you tell the teacher he won't listen, he just says "little liar", but it's not true, I'm not a liar! Don't you believe me, Uncle?'

'I believe you, Antoine.'

He's happy now, and starts jumping about, while behind me I hear a shy little girl's voice:

'Uncle, I want a dress like Ursula's!'

'Who's Ursula?'

'I can't tell you. There are too many people here, they'll tease me…'

'Whisper it in my ear, then…'

I signal to the others to move off a bit, and I bend forward till I'm down at little Julie's height. She puts her mouth right next to my ear and hisses:

'Ursula's a bad girl! She's my enemy…'

'Your enemy?'

'Yeah, she pinched my boyfriend because her father bought her a red dress with yellow flowers on. I want the same dress so my boyfriend will love me too…'

As she's speaking right into my ear, I answer right back into hers. This game makes the others jealous, I can tell from the frowns on most of their faces. They reckon Julie's getting special treatment, and they all want to talk to me like this, but I straighten up again.

They shout out a litany of lists. Each time I say yes, the lists get longer. Some requests are quite reasonable, like Célestin's:

'I want some Kojak sweets.'

Another has more contemporary tastes:

'I want a video game I saw on the TV yesterday!'

One of the cocky ones pushes the group aside:

'Uncle, I'm the brainiest here! You have to get me a laptop computer!…'

Another contradicts him:

'He's lying, Uncle, he never listens, he had to repeat his last two years of primary! I'm the brainiest, and I want to go to France and America with you!'

I don't know exactly how many of them there are, and I've no idea when they were all born. They aren't all here. Some are only a year apart, or even a few months. Every day new ones are added to the long list I was given when I arrived in town.

The mother of a nephew I don't recognise pushes her son towards me:

'His name's Jaden, you'd better not leave him out!'

This nephew is hiding behind his mother, I can just see the gleam of his eyes.

'Go on, Jaden, tell Uncle what you want him to buy you!'

Jaden is overwhelmed now, he sucks on his thumb and whines:

'A car…'

'OK, I'll get you a toy tomorrow when I go into town,' I tell him.

At this his eyes widen and he takes his thumb out of his mouth.

'No, I want a car like grown-ups have, with a real horn, otherwise I'll make an accident, and someone will die!'

His mother strokes his head:

'Jaden, you're too little to drive a big person's car…'

'Doesn't matter if I'm little! I still want a car, I can keep it till I'm big…'

Cornered, the mother says:

'Uncle will buy you one and put it in a garage in France for you. They look after cars in France, they never get stolen there. And when you're grown up you can go and fetch it yourself. In a real plane!'

But he's a cunning one, and shakes his head in disbelief:

'No, when he leaves he won't come back again!'

'Why do you say that?' his mother says.

'You told me, you said when this uncle goes travelling he stays with the whites for twenty years and doesn't come back, and I'll be as old as Papa in twenty years. And Papa's old already, and he doesn't have a car…'

Even when it's not clear how we are related, they all call me *tonton*, uncle, and no one seems to mind, especially not the parents. Since I never had a brother or a sister, this gives me an unaccountable sense of pride. I don't know them, and I will forget most of their faces once I get back in the plane. Little Jaden is probably right: how many have left, and never returned, or returned only twenty years later? Every household in the town can probably claim one.

Still, I need to learn to recognise these little angels, and get their names straight, or they'll be offended. Even if I've never seen them before, I feel close to them, and I know there's a drop of my blood in their veins. The ones I do know slightly are the children of Gilbert, and of Bienvenüe, who is still in hospital, and whose absence is keenly felt at home. Their children insist on having their photo taken with me. And they choose, by chance, the same spot where I used to sit with Gilbert and Bienvenüe to eat. Here's where Aunt Mâ Ngudi used to punish me for not finishing what was on my plate, where I toyed with my foufou balls, playing for time. And yet you could tell she really loved me. It was her that told my uncle one day that it wasn't me wetting the bed, it was my cousin. My uncle was sceptical about this, so Mâ Ngudi then carried out an experiment which to Gilbert felt like the greatest mortification of his life. He was made to sleep alone in the room, while Bienvenüe and I slept in the living room. The next day the evidence spoke for itself: Gilbert, in terror of the three-headed monster, had once again pissed in the bed…

Whenever I was really naughty at home, my mother took me to Mâ Ngudi's and told her I wouldn't eat, that I was doing the 'only child' thing, as she put it. My aunt gave me a defiant look, then turned to my mother:

'He'll eat in this house, Pauline, don't you worry, I'll make sure of it. If he gets up to any tricks I'll send him over to eat Grandma Hélène's huge portions!'

Mâ Ngudi set to work making a beef soup and foufou balls. I wanted to slip away, but her fierce glare kept me rooted to the spot, and I stayed in the yard, right where my little nieces and nephews are sitting for the photo. Mâ Ngudi set a steaming plate of food, and a bowl of foufou down in front of me. I simply wasn't hungry, but I had to eat, because my aunt had a rubber whip in her hands. I swallowed great mouthfuls, without feeling them go down into my stomach. I held back my tears, but suddenly felt the need to cough. I began to vomit, while Mâ Ngudi whipped me, and yelled at me to finish my food. I was used to seeing her wave a whip around. I'd stand there before her, eyes cast down in submission. You hardly ever caught her smiling. She was only ever radiant when Uncle Albert was around. It never lasted long, and we felt she was somehow never satisfied, even if everything was fine and we'd all eaten well, there was the washing up to do, the yard to sweep, the bottles on deposit to return to the bar in the Avenue of Independence. She wasn't particularly hard on me, she treated her own children exactly the same, whipping them with a force that quite alarmed me. Whenever this happened, and I expected to be given the same punishment as them, since we had all been in it together, I feared the worst. But she tempered her lashes, reminding me, perhaps, that I wasn't her child, that there were limits to her anger. Which Gilbert and Bienvenüe considered an injustice. My cousin always took it out on me once her mother had gone. She would pinch my ears and growl:

'I'm pulling your great long ears, since Maman didn't whip you like us!'

I met a friend from France in the lobby of the French Institute and showed him the photo of me with my nephews and nieces, and he remarked that they, 'like most children in Pointe-Noire', lived in a 'paradise of poverty'. A native of Pointe-Noire himself, he launched into the kind of speech you hear from people who have lived so long in Europe, they now accept the image of the black continent projected by the media. While he was having his say, I watched him pityingly. He had forgotten where he came from, and had come to believe that the introduction of European ways would bring happiness to our country. He doesn't seem to realise that the chains that bind him in what he believes to be a comfortable life in Europe hold no attraction for my little tribe over in the rue du Louboulou. True, he wears a suit and tie and polished shoes every day, when he's back here. But whenever I meet him in Europe he's dressed quite differently. Here he plays a role: broadcasting the notion that the salvation of every Congolese lies over in Europe. Back there he comes face to face with reality, which he won't be sharing with the young people wandering the streets of Pointe-Noire: he lives in less than twenty square metres, must struggle to legitimise his presence in France, and gets up every morning to go in search of casual work.

These children, though, find points of light in the harshness of their lives. It took me a while to understand that they were just as happy as I was when I was their age, and found my happiness in a plate of hot food in the kitchen, in the growing grass, in the tweeting of a couple of courting birds, or in the poster for an Indian film showing at the Rex cinema, where we started queuing at ten in the morning in the hope of getting into the three o'clock showing. The difficulties of our parents' lives were something quite distant, and besides, we had confidence in them, they cleverly concealed their anxieties, the shortages, the difficulty of getting through to the end of the month, so as not to spoil our childish innocence.

Thinking back to my childhood, when we hid in the lantana fields near the Agostinho Neto airport and hunted iridescent beetles or fished for minnows from the banks of the River Tchinouka, I replied to my friend, with his 'Parisian Negro' arrogance:

'These children aren't in a paradise of poverty. Here, look at the photo: that tyre, those flip-flops... that's what makes them happy... flip-flops to walk in, the tyre they can all climb aboard like a motorbike big enough to carry all their wildest dreams. Every day my nephews and nieces walk out in a long line down the rue du Louboulou. Their childhood knits them together, they wouldn't swap it for all the world. They drink from a small glass, but it's their own. Your glass is big, but it's not yours, and each time you want to drink from it, you have to ask for permission. And alas, that permission is never granted...

The ladykillers

His real name is Alphonse Bikindou, but we call him by his nickname, though no one knows what it means or where it comes from: Grand Poupy.

I meet him this afternoon at my mother's place and it seems his face has not a wrinkle, and that he'll stay exactly as I've always known him till the day he dies: quite small, a prominent forehead, narrow eyes sparkling with intelligence and cunning. He now has a thin moustache, and to take myself back to when I was a kid, only slightly younger than him, I try to ignore his facial hair, which puts a barrier between us. He is my mother's cousin, and moved to Pointe-Noire from the country in the late 1970s, to live with us and go to the lycée. The very first day I saw him, I was captivated by his deep voice and his way of articulating almost every word separately. I started secondary school just as he started at the lycée, and we'd get up in the morning and put on our school uniforms, him all in khaki, with long trousers, me in a sky-blue shirt and dark blue shorts, and a red 'pioneers of the Congolese Revolution' kerchief round my neck. I always lagged behind him, and every now and then he would turn round, so I'd have to hurry to catch him up. I could never manage it, his little legs had a kind of almost mechanical strength despite the way the road seemed to get steeper and steeper, so that we would overtake other pupils sitting exhausted by the wayside. A bit farther on, at the junction of the Avenue Jean-Felix-Tchicaya and the rue Jacques-Opangault, where we went our separate ways, he would act the big brother – he was no longer a minor – and tell me to mind the traffic and hand me a twenty-five CFA franc coin:

'Buy yourself some fritters and mash at break. Watch the big kids don't steal your money.'

As he walked off, I'd stand and watch him for a moment, making his way down to the far end of the avenue to where the Karl Marx lycée stood. After a few minutes he was no more than a tiny speck, absorbed into the crowd of students. Then off I went to the Trois Glorieuses secondary school. I arrived just in time for the raising of the flag in the schoolyard, when we all sang the national anthem, which we were made to learn by heart:

Arise, brave country,
Who, in three glorious days,
Seized the flag and raised it
for a Congo, new and free
That never more will stumble
And no more be afraid.

Our chains we have burst open,
Now freely we will work
We are one sovereign nation.

If my foes do slay me,
Before my hour has come,
Brave comrade, take my gun;
And if a bullet hits my heart
Our sisters all will fearless rise,

Hills, river, too, with all their might
Will repel the invader.

Today our land is born anew,
And all in value equal,
No leader but the people,
Who alone has chosen
To stand in dignity.

Grand Poupy favoured white shirts and terylene trousers, which he ironed energetically every weekend. He cut his own hair, in the style of the Afro-American actors of the 1970s, whose posters we fought over on the Avenue of Independence, where they were laid out for sale on the ground outside the Rex, the Duo and the Roy.

The layout of the interior of our three-room house changed with the arrival of my mother's cousin. By now it was a really tight squeeze, with my aunts Sabine Bouanga and N'Soni in one room, and my parents in the other. Any other member of the family who happened to turn up had to find a corner in the living room to lay down a mat, without getting too close to where Uncle Mompéro had set up his bed and would not be moved. Grand Poupy's arrival would upset my routine. I no longer slept with my uncle, and chose instead to share the mat with the latest arrival, listen to him relate amorous escapades, which of course always ended with victory for him and the surrender of his lady-love, as long as Uncle Mompéro didn't complain and tell us to shut up. Grand Poupy would lower his voice, while my uncle ranted from his bed:

'I can hear you, Poupy, you're keeping me awake! If you don't shut up I'll wake up the boy's mother and you can explain yourself to her! Ever since you got here you've been filling his head with your lies! Has anyone ever seen these girls you're always boasting about?'

At this point Grand Poupy would whisper to me:

'Let's go to sleep, I'll tell you the rest tomorrow. Uncle Mompéro doesn't know Grand Poupy, ladies' man extraordinaire!'

On days when there was no school, he would suggest we take a walk in the neighbourhood:

'I'll show you how to approach a girl, just watch what I do! As soon as I see a girl, I'll go up and talk to her. There's one sign that's always a giveaway: if I put my hand on her right shoulder and she doesn't remove it, things are looking good…'

We were standing at an intersection about two hundred yards from the house, a strategic spot from which we could see most of the girls in the Vongou neighbourhood pass by. They were on their way to market, some dressed in multicoloured pagnes, others in tight-fitting trousers, with tops that bordered on indecent. If my mother's cousin liked the look of one of them, he would turn up the collar of his shirt, smooth his Afro with the palm of his hand, and quickly spray some perfume under his armpits, behind his ears and even inside his mouth:

'Don't move, I'm coming back!'

He'd set off after the girl, imitating almost to the point of caricature the manner of Aldo Maccione, who he'd seen in *L'Aventure c'est l'aventure*.

I watched from a distance as Grand Poupy hitched up his trousers, smiling his broadest smile and finally placing his hand on the girl's right shoulder. He would turn back to me and wink. Seeing his conquest didn't shake off his hand, I decided Grand Poupy must be right, he was an ace, and his technique was infallible. What would have happened if the young lady had removed his hand? I had complete faith in his ability to come up with a response. He'd probably already encountered more difficult cases, and knew instinctively which girls he could target and be sure of success. So, I decided, he wouldn't risk it if he thought there was a chance he'd be rejected. Why, for instance, did he tend to go for the ugly ones, when a real beauty might be passing just a few centimetres away, flashing us her most provocative smile? If I ventured to question him on this matter, he would say, with an air of great experience:

'A smile isn't enough, you have to wait till she touches her hair, and especially till she looks down at the ground. Did she do that, the beauty who went by a couple of minutes ago?'

'No...'

'Well then, that's why I didn't waste my energy! I'm telling you, the pretty ones are only interested in the boys who don't notice them. They want to be seen, that's what they're aiming for. And another thing, if you meet two girls together, an ugly one with a pretty one, I mean, start with the ugly one, and the pretty one will start flirting with you the next day, just as a challenge to the other one. I call it the billiard technique: to get to a ball and pocket it you need to hit another one, and fortunately it's possible to hit two birds with one stone, because both balls could end up in the same pocket, or in two different holes! But that takes experience, and you're still a beginner...'

'And if both of them are pretty, which ball do you aim for?'

'Impossible! There'll always be one prettier than the other, there's no such thing as a draw in beauty, or in ugliness either!'

Sometimes, when he wasn't looking, I'd open the notebook where he wrote down the girls' names, with some of them marked 'to simmer'.

Intrigued, I plunged in one evening:

'So what does it mean, to simmer?'

Grand Poupy gave a start, and his face expressed grave disappointment:

'So, how long have you been looking through my private things?'

He had raised his voice, and just as I began to feel tears pricking my eyes, he spoke more softly, to console me:

'No point snivelling now… What's done is done. Don't do it again. I'll tell you what "leave to simmer" means…'

He took out the notebook from his satchel and opened it:

'On the left-hand page I write out the names of the girls I've already been out with, and the right-hand page is for the ones I'm still working on. Some of them are the tricky ones I've already tried it with, I've kissed them on the lips, but they put on an act, they don't want me to go any farther. So I pretend I'm not interested in them, like I haven't got time for them, I let them simmer, like a dish you cook over a low heat in a pot. It pays off eventually because in the end those are the girls that come running after me! And I'm back in charge!'

I wasn't honest with my mother's cousin, I continued to read his notebook without him knowing. I discovered it wasn't just the names of his sweethearts he wrote down. He also recorded his memories of Sibiti, the place he came from. I remember long passages without a single crossing out, in which he described the adventures of a certain Chelos, to whom the writing was addressed. They all began the same way:

'My dear, true friend, dear Chelos, As the moon is my witness, I am sending you another story from my little backwater of Sibiti…'

I wondered whether this Chelos person really existed or was just a product of his mischievous imagination. Grand Poupy wrote at night, when everyone else was asleep. He lit a candle, opened a school exercise book, took a ballpoint pen and covered the empty pages with black ink at breathtaking speed. The stories were mostly bawdy, particularly the one about a woman called Massika, and her lover, Bosco. Massika had assured Bosco that her husband was away at a funeral in a neighbouring village. He wouldn't be back till the end of the morning of the following day. So, that evening, Bosco turned up and sat down to eat with Massika. The two love pigeons got drunk on palm wine and laughed together like hyenas. In the middle of the night they disappeared into the bedroom and began making love when suddenly there was a loud knocking at the door. Massika couldn't think who it might be at that hour of the night. She must either open the door or do nothing and wait for the night visitor to go away. But he knocked louder and louder, and began shouting Massika's name, till she realised it must be her man standing out there.

'Come and open the door, I can't find my key!'

'I thought you went to the wake?'

'I'll explain later, first open the door.'

Bosco just had time to slip under the bed as the door opened and the man of the house put down his bag in the main room. He complained his feet were sore, and asked his wife to go and boil some water for him. When she came back and set a steaming bucket down before her husband he picked it up without a word, slipped into the bedroom with it and emptied it out under the bed. Bosco, who was stark naked, burst out of his hiding place, pushed past the husband, got as far as the main room and plunged out of the front door, followed by the adulterous wife. The two vanished in the darkness while in the distance you could hear the barking of dogs, who must have been having a laugh at their expense, two humans, dressed like Adam and Eve…

The truth was, Grand Poupy dreamed of being a writer…

Here's Grand Poupy now. We embrace. Behind him I see a woman whose face is vaguely familiar. I hold out my hand to her tentatively, and my mother's cousin looks almost shocked:

'You're going to shake her hand? Won't you kiss her? Why so formal? Don't you recognise her?'

I take another look. The woman smiles at me. I can see in her face, she's a bit disappointed. She's come to my mother's plot, where Grand Poupy and I have arranged to meet, specially to see me. It was actually my mother's cousin who insisted she come today because she hadn't been able to make it to the family reunion, she was babysitting.

'Go on, kiss her, it's Alphonsine!'

I start at the name. Memories flood back, and Grand Poupy's teasing smile and Alphonsine's now beaming face make me realise how stupid I've been. I can see her now as she was back then, braiding my mother's hair. I was too shy to come out of this hut, because I was in love with her. Grand Poupy bombarded me with advice, told me just to jump in and swim, wrote out what I had to say to her when we met. I was so paralysed by Alphonsine, face to face with her, I went to pieces, and started to stammer. She was troubled, too, and would run off when I finally managed to put Grand Poupy's tips into practice, placing my hand on her shoulder. I sent her poems, letters which he read and corrected, and which even so received no reply. In this passionate, one-way correspondence I described her eyes, shimmering, yet moist, her fair skin, like clay fashioned by an archangel who had leaned over her cradle without her parents knowing. These letters were delivered personally by my mother's cousin. At least, that's what he swore when got back, with a smile on his lips, jeering at my cowardice. Alphonsine was well ready for me, he claimed, I had better hurry up or some scoundrel would come and put a spoke in the wheels.

'You'll have only yourself to blame!' he warned.

I advanced at a tortoise-like pace in this relationship, to which I attributed all my adolescent angst. As far as I recall I never managed to be with Alphonsine and say anything coherent for more than about ten minutes. In my late teens I was living in Brazzaville and she was back in Pointe-Noire. We lost track of each other, resigned to a platonic relationship, without even a little kiss.

And here she is now right in front of me, a grown-up lady, with two children standing up straight behind her. Grand Poupy smiles impishly. Finally he cracks and bursts out laughing:

'See, my boy, Alphonsine is one of the family now, I went a different way about it: I married her myself, and we've got children. So, they are your nephews, you must look after them as if they were your own children. We live in M'Paka, on the outskirts of town. One of our daughters, the oldest, is studying in Morocco…'

I burst out laughing too, and say:

'Who's the sly one, eh, Grand Poupy! There you were, pretending to give me advice, and all the time you were putting your own case!'

Alphonsine avoids my eye.

'Hey, Grand Poupy, Alphonsine's looking at the ground, she's touching her hair, what does that mean, then?'

Another peal of laughter from my cousin.

'Little rascal! You haven't forgotten, then!'

As we make our way to my mother's castle, I ask him:

'What happened to your friend Chelos? You know, if you've still got those manuscripts, I can help you find a publisher in France and...'

'Forget it, my boy, I don't have that tapeworm in my gut that writers have, that eats away at their insides every day. Writing's hard, but what's even harder is knowing you'll never be a writer, living with the idea you might have left something marvellous behind when you go. I love to read what you publish, you've become what I would have liked to be: a public storyteller. I don't know what you'll scribble down after this meeting, but with you I know to expect the worst, you got me perfectly in *Black Bazaar*... And when the kids here read it, they think I can still help them with chat-up lines!...'

My uncle

Uncle Mompéro is considered the 'doyen' of the family, since my mother passed on. He takes his role seriously, and no one would dare challenge his status. From the doorway of the solid built house – the one on which Maman Pauline had started the work, which was carried on and completed by my cousins – he watches the comings and goings in the yard. It is not unusual to hear him raise his voice, demand silence, or tick off the kids who are squabbling. Whenever a car goes past the house, he leaps out of his easy chair, checking that the little ones are safe. Equally, a noisy crowd will arouse his curiosity at once, shaking him from his torpor, to intervene if necessary. I saw all this today when I was chatting with my cousin Kihouari: he crept up on us, appeared in the doorway, then went back off into the main room to wait for me to come and see him once I had finished with the others…

Each time a stranger arrives on our plot he thinks it's going to be bad news, and brutally poses the same question:

'Who's dead this time?'

The visitor will notice his air of worry and despair, no doubt because of all the sisters and brothers who've departed over the last twenty years: Uncle Albert, Aunt Sabine, Maman Pauline, Aunt Dorothée and Uncle René.

I'm facing him, and he knows I have no bad news to bring

him. He wears a circumspect smile I find deeply touching, with his face only very slightly marked with expression lines between his eyebrows and his forehead. I suspect him of having cut his hair specially to look 'tidy' in front of me. Even his black shoes are spotless, as though he didn't touch the ground when he walked. He's sporting a fine white shirt with wide beige stripes.

My mother never got to grow any grey hairs. But looking at my uncle I can imagine roughly what her scalp would have looked like if she had lived to be over sixty, like him. I am sure she wouldn't have been one of those old ladies who spend the day sitting out in front of their houses. She'd still be on the go, selling her peanuts at the Grand Marché, where lots of elderly women still ply this trade, some of them dozing behind their stalls. If Maman Pauline saw me turn up here now, she would fling herself at me, with a huge smile that would make me believe she could get the better of time itself. That's the impression Uncle Mompéro would like to give me too, today. He'll say nothing of his state of health, which is declining, or of everything he's endured these last twenty-three years, during which we have been out of touch. Now, Grand Poupy had already mentioned to me that our uncle wasn't well, that he had undergone an operation for appendicitis, that the moment I turned my back he would suddenly age, facing the sawing pain of his poorly treated illness. I was astonished and protested that my uncle appeared to be in good health. Grand Poupy had at once grown serious:

'When he heard you were coming back to Pointe-Noire, he put his illness to one side, to put a brave face on it. He's like your mother, when she was hospitalised at Adolphe-Sicé, she ordered us to tell you nothing till she was dead. Uncle Mompéro isn't in such good shape as you think, he won't tell you, but don't ask him, or he'll never forgive us…'

My uncle begins to talk to me, his head tilted up towards the ceiling, which, I remember, indicates I mustn't interrupt him:

'I haven't changed, you know, I'm still the same man who held your hand through the night when you were terrified of the dark and thought it was full of man-eating ghosts from the tombs in the Mont-Kamba cemetery, coming to attack children. Your mother's gone now, but she still lives, through me, and she's left me enough breath in my lungs to wait for you, the time it took. Your rendezvous with her never happened; ours, thanks be to God, has happened. It didn't happen by chance, you mustn't blame yourself that you weren't here when we mourned for my sister. I knew you were grieving too, wherever you were, I know everything that happens in your body, and in your spirit. The truth is, to me, you're not a nephew, but my own son, the child I never had, the child I never will have now, because the older I get, the more I realise that I was put on this earth to protect the person my sister loved above everyone and everything: you. I never wanted descendants of my own, in case it took me away from you, and you considered me more as an uncle than a true father. I don't want to be your uncle, I am your father! Was it an accident your biological father abandoned you? You should tell yourself now, you've been lucky to have three men in your life. The first one failed in his mission to be a father, and ran off just before you were born, you can wipe him from your mind, you have already, it's better that way, lowlife like him don't deserve respect, since they never showed any themselves. The second – your stepfather, Roger – was a generous man, who took you in, you and your mother. You must honour him, so that all adopted children, everywhere, know their life is not doomed to failure, just because their father was an idiot. I am the third man, completing the trinity of your fate. Do you not hear the sweet music of your mother's voice when I speak to you? You may wander far from me, as you have done until now, but I will still be there, sometimes just sitting watching time flow by, but mostly wandering along the banks of patience, whatever the force of the gales. I'll blow with all my breath on the embers of time itself to be able to stay on this earth just long enough to see you take over the reins of this shattered family, with all its internal divisions, that are hidden from you. Look at these people! They put on a united front, but when you scratch the surface you discover all this hostility, that I have to contend with. You've got one person accusing another of causing his father or mother's death, and others fighting over land left by my brother Albert Moukila in the 1970s! Is that what you call a family? That's what killed your uncle René, other people's greed, even if it has to be said he didn't exactly set a good example, grabbing the house that should have gone to your cousins Gilbert and Bienvenüe! I'll forgive him that, though it is a pity the house was sold secretly by my older sister Sabine Bouanga's son, with not a single centime going to Albert's own children! I'm looking to you now to get your bleach out and do a proper clean-up in this family. Don't be too nice about it, they'd think you were just being weak, and you'd pay with your life. I'm exhausted, totally exhausted, I'm sick of battling on all alone. You're here now, and here I am, where I was when you left me. But I won't be next time, you know. I'll be gone too, gone to join my sister Pauline…'

In the silence that follows I sense that he wants to describe my mother's last days, and is looking for the right words, or rather, wondering how to begin. He's seen my face grow troubled, and he stops himself. We leave that chapter unopened, though it's there in both our minds.

We leave the main house and go over to my mother's castle. Outside the shack he turns to me and shows me his hands:

'These are the hands that built this place, remember? You helped me a bit, you really wanted to be useful! The house isn't the same now, there's only half of it left, I had to cut the other part off when your mother died. I couldn't bear to see the room she slept in…

He strokes the planks thoughtfully:

These planks speak to me at night… Do you know the same are used to make coffins?'

I nod my head. He was a great joiner in his day, and made the frames of many of the houses in this town. I never liked it when he made coffins and the bereaved families waited around outside his workshop.

I reach out and touch the planks too. Pleased by my gesture, he immediately says:

'Yes, touch them, they're glad to see you. They know who we are, they were there at the start. Whenever they moan it makes me think your mother's suffering up there, and wants me to come and join her…'

I still don't interrupt the flow of what seem like thoughts he's been saving up for a long time now, for the day he could whisper them to me.

'It seems like death's had it in for us,' he goes on. 'Maybe there's a curse on this patch of land, because of the way I treated Miguel. Night and day I think of the misery I inflicted on that dog…'

An image of Miguel pops into my head. I hear him barking, then whimpering with thirst and hunger. Once the link between myself and my imaginary sisters, he died at the foot of the mango tree that used to dominate the plot. Did the neighbours hear his desperate cries? And this tree, witness to the scene, why didn't it set the poor beast free? Maman Pauline was crazy about Miguel, he was a present from one of her girlfriends who just wanted to get rid of the litter of puppies. People said she had so many dogs she sometimes threw some into the River Tchinouka. I was the one who thought of the name Miguel for our new arrival, who steadily grew each time I filled his bowl with milk. Feeding the dog was like a game for me, and he followed me round the whole day long, hoping for his next feed. He listened to me with his ears pricked up, and answered by wagging his tail like wind-screen wipers. I'd learned to reckon a dog's age with him. Within a single year he was older than me, almost twice my age. I was proud to fix a sign at the entrance to the plot that said 'Beware of the dog.' I walked with him round the backstreets of the Voungou neighbourhood, confident he would be my constant protector. Alas, when some children my age threw stones at us, Miguel opted to hide behind me rather than go and bite them as he would have done if we had been at home and someone had come and attacked us. I realised that most dogs were only brave inside the boundaries of their master's home. So often I had seen our dog, who was so timid when we were out and about, fling himself around the yard in a frenzy with his tail between his legs, barking his head off outside the house, fit to burst our eardrums. I loved him in spite of this, and he returned my love, licking my little hands with his tongue, or standing up on his two feet. Our happiness was not to last. My mother went away for a month and I was sent, for the first time, to stay with my mother's military brother, Jean-Marie Moulounda, in Brazzaville. Papa Roger was at Maman Martine's. The whole house was practi-cally empty; Grand Poupy was at Sibiti and the various aunts had gone back to Louboulou to work in the fields. Only Uncle

Mompéro was left, and my mother had asked him to look after Miguel, to feed him three times a day and take him for walks so he could do his business outside our plot. My uncle did this for two or three days. Then he left town himself to go and work on a site in Dolisie, the third-biggest town in the country, over three hundred kilometres from Pointe-Noire, where they were building a primary school. Instead of letting the dog wander free on our land, for a few days he had kept him tied up with a piece of rope to the foot of the mango tree, where he came and gave him his food and water, as Maman Pauline had asked. The day of his departure for Dolisie, my uncle forgot about Miguel and left him captive. On his return, a few hours before his sister, the poor beast was no longer of this world. Papa Roger and Maman Pauline cried murder. They considered trying to hide Miguel's death from me. But they knew that when I got back from Brazzaville the next day, the first thing I would ask was: 'Where's Miguel?'

Uncle Mompéro suggested buying another dog. My mother was against this. She did not wish to sully the memory of Miguel, and added that if they hadn't been capable of looking after one dog, there was no reason to think they would do better with the next one.

When I got home, I was given to believe that Miguel had succumbed to a heart attack. Naively, I replied:

'But dogs don't die of heart attacks, because they don't have all those problems in the heart that humans have.'

Uncle Mompéro took me to one side and told me the truth:

'You were right, my boy, dogs don't die of heart attacks... Miguel died because of my stupidity. I'm an imbecile, I accept that. When I left for Dolisie I completely forgot we had a dog, and that I'd tied him up. If I'd only left him unattached he would have survived. But it's my fault, please don't hate me for it. Your mother doesn't want me to buy another dog, but if you want I'll buy you one anyway…'

'Don't buy another dog…'

'But why not?'

'Because we didn't buy Miguel… he was given to us. And anyway, when someone dies do you buy someone else to replace them?'

'I could go and see the woman who gave your mother Miguel and if her dog's had some more puppies we'd at least have a puppy from the same family as Miguel and…'

'No, it was Miguel I loved, I don't want another dog in my life, then when I think of dogs, I'll only ever think of him…'

Uncle Mompéro fixes a plank that's come loose from the shack, and turns to me:

'That's right, *mon petit*, Miguel's always with me, as your mother is. When we had the first family reunion I couldn't speak about him in front of everyone. It's just the two of us today, face to face, please forgive me, help me wipe this curse away, I'm going down on my knees now…'

He goes down on one knee, and before he can get down on both I stop him:

'No, Uncle, don't do that, there's no curse on this plot…'

'How do you know? Animals are our relatives, our doubles, you said so in your book about the porcupine…'

'I was only reporting what Maman used to tell me. There are friendly doubles, too, Miguel was one of those, he's forgiven you for what you did…'

A smile appears on his face:

'And do you forgive me too?'

'I never held it against you for one moment, Uncle!'

He wipes his eyes with the back of his right hand. Tears no doubt released by my removal of this thorn from his foot.

We go back to the main house.

This is my third visit, but this time there's no family reunion. Before I leave the plot, my uncle adopts a solemn air and says:

'Are you already going back to where the whites are putting you up in the centre of town? My brother Matété looked for you there yesterday, they said you were out all the time. It's very important, he wants to see you alone. Just agree to what he asks, he and I have talked about it… Will you leave me at least five thousand CFA francs? I just need to buy some little things like razors, toothpaste, soap…'

I smile at him as I take the notes from my pocket.

Close encounters of the third kind

There's a knock at the door, I open it, and find Uncle Matété standing there. He's come with a little bunch of bananas, which he puts down in the middle of the room. I pick it up and take it through to the kitchen, while he looks round my rooms, with undisguised amazement.

'Do the whites pay for you to stay in this place?'

I explain that the French Institute invited me to attend a conference for a few days, and I decided to extend my stay, to see the family, and write a book.

'And how much do you pay to stay here?' he replies, going out on to the balcony.

'They make this apartment available for writers and artists, I don't pay anything.'

'I came yesterday, it's hard to get hold of you, I must have been back three times! This is all very nice, isn't it?'

Without waiting for my reply, he points over at the building opposite:

'Look, even at night you can see the Adolphe-Sicé hospital really clearly! Have you visited Bienvenüe there yet?'

'No…'

'I don't blame you. You're scared of Room One too, I guess?

Anyone who goes in, even just to visit, will end up there one day to die…'

By night the hospital looks like a huge haunted manor house, with dim, uneven lighting issuing from the few windows still left open. Uncle Matété suddenly falls silent. He passes his hand over his close-cropped skull, which gleams with the light from the moon emerged from the dark clouds cast over the town. I imagine what he must thinking, how far his thoughts will take him. His eyebrows are quite grey and I sometimes think he looks older than Uncle Mompéro, who he gets on well with, and who was the one who told me he would be coming to see me, though I hadn't been sure it would be today, this evening. They are both the children of Grandfather Grégoire Moukila, by different mothers.

I guess Uncle Matété's thinking back to when I was a child in Louboulou village. I was around ten years old, and it was my first time in the bush. The second day of my visit, he decided to take me hunting with him, despite my mother's objections, and my grandmother N'Soko's indignation. Grandfather Moukila intervened to reassure everyone:

'Let them go, they'll be all right, my spirits will watch over them. After all, the boy needs to go there, before it's too late…'

I have never forgotten our nocturnal escapade. I arrived home on my uncle's shoulders, my legs scraped raw with scratches and grazes, my face covered in insect bites. Uncle Matété borrowed Grandfather's shotgun and we left at the dead of night. Some time before leaving, we smeared our faces with ashes, a technique designed, he said, to catch the wild animals off guard, by convincing them we were of their kind. Next, round our ankles, we tied grasses I still don't know the names of, to ward off any snakes we met on our way. We followed a winding path that my uncle knew like the back of his hand, till, after a few kilometres, we reached a stream burbling between rocks. At the edge of the stream he gave a sign to show I shouldn't speak, not even whisper or squash a biting mosquito. A hundred or so metres from us a hind and a stag were drinking. I waited for my uncle to take up his position and shoot down at least one of them. But instead he knelt on the ground and began chanting words I didn't understand. The two grazing animals watched us from a distance, but seemed untroubled by our presence. Uncle Matété's prayer seemed to go on for ever, interspersed with names of people in our family like at school when the teacher was checking we were all present before starting lessons. Except that no one answered my uncle's name-call. The two deer listened carefully to his monotonous speech, nodding their heads in agreement every now and then. When the prayer was finished, the two mammals bellowed loudly then began to move off from the water, eventually vanishing into the depths of the bush. The silence in their wake was chilling. My uncle knew what I was thinking, and got in first:

'I'll explain tomorrow, for now just follow me, we need to find something to take back home. We can cross the river now, we've got permission…'

We went on deeper and deeper into the forest and when I turned around, Uncle Matété whispered:

'Never look over your shoulder in the bush…'

'But we'll get lost, we won't know how to get home again,' I worried.

'Have you ever seen anyone get lost in his own home?'

'But what if it was a big house, like the white people's castles?'

'Well, the difference is, this is our castle, we know it, it doesn't just belong to one family like it does in the white people's land, it belongs to all the villagers.'

We came out into a clearing and heard a noise coming from the top of a palm tree. My uncle swung his torch towards it. It was a pair of squirrels, one on top of the other, absorbed in a courtship ritual which was shaking the leaves of the tree. The bang from my uncle's gun made my ears pop. Both animals had been hit with a single bullet. Uncle Matété picked them up from the bottom of the tree and put them in his game bag.

A bit farther on, an anteater was curled up in a ball in the middle of the path. This species is renowned for its poor eyesight, but as soon as the torchlight caught him, he lifted his snout and tried to make a run for it. Too late: my uncle had already taken aim and squeezed the trigger. The bullet blew out the creature's brains.

'Right, we can go back now, that's enough for this evening,' he decided.

It seemed a long way home. It felt as though the weeds were slashing at my legs, and leaving my uncle's untouched. I could hardly keep upright, and complained now of mosquitoes and other insects flying into my eyes. Some of these seemed to flash and then zoom in on me so fast I thought they must be shooting stars falling out of the sky. Uncle Matété told me to walk in front of him. After a few metres he noticed I was slowing us down. At this speed it would take us five or six hours to get back to the village. At first he teased me, calling me a town boy, then he lifted me over his head while I slipped my legs round his neck. My right foot rubbed against his well-stocked game bag, which he wore like a shoulder bag. Even in this more comfort-able position I sometimes had to bend low to avoid the branches sticking out from the trees, and the little fluorescent creatures who must know I was just a town boy, the way they picked on me.

Back in the village I lay awake the rest of the night. I was in a sweat, haunted by visions of the hind and stag. I saw them standing there, the male with a human head, crowned with branched horns whose tips just touched the clouds, the female a little apart. The two of them spoke our language, and said my name. The pair had a fawn following after them now, and the little animal's head looked exactly like mine! What's more, he kept giggling for no reason, and his parents didn't stop him.

I was up early next morning, at dawn: I ran into my uncle's bedroom, while he was still snoring. He awoke with a start, and didn't seem in the least surprised at my bursting in so early:

'You've come to tell me about the hind and the stag! You want to tell me you saw them in a dream?'

'Yes…'

'Well then! Now they know you! How did they appear to you?'

'They were with their child, and the child had my face! He was laughing like a mad thing, I don't laugh like that…'

'I'd expect that, the child was happy to see you, because you and he are one body. The hind and the stag weren't just ordinary animals. The male is the double of your grandfather, Moukila Grégoire, and the female is the double of your grandmother, Henriette N'Soko. If I had killed those creatures when we were out hunting yesterday, your grandparents would be dead by now. Before you enter the bush you have to go and say good evening to the doubles, then they help us find our game. People who don't respect this ritual always come home empty-handed, or get lost in the forest. Or not lost exactly, but they get turned into trees or into stones by the spirits of the bush. When you're grown up, whatever bush you go into, remind yourself that spirits live there, and be respectful of the fauna and the flora, including objects that seem unimportant to you, like mushrooms, or the lowly little earthworm trying to climb back on to the riverbank. In our family we only hunt squirrels and anteaters, those are the prey given us by our ancestors, because the other animals, unless we are expressly told otherwise in our dreams, are members of our family who've left this world, but are still living in the next. Would you eat your mother, your father or your brother? I think not. I know these things sound strange to you, you've grown up in the city, but they are simple truths that make us who we are. Now, you mustn't eat hind or stag meat, because even if it didn't kill you, a part of you would disappear, the part we call *luck* or, rather, *blessing.*'

I gave a little cough behind Uncle Matété, as he stood there looking out at the Adolphe-Sicé hospital. He turned round and asked me very seriously:

'Tell me truthfully: have you ever eaten hind or stag meat?'

'No!'

'That is a relief, nephew, you did listen to me, then! You can't imagine how I worried about you!'

We go back into the living room. Since he arrived unannounced, I've nothing to offer him. In the kitchen I find three eggs, which I break and throw into a pan. I break off three bananas from the bunch he gave me. While I'm busy making the food, I feel his presence behind me.

'Nephew, what are you doing?'

'I'm making you something to eat.'

'No, no, don't do that… In any case, I don't eat eggs, and you can't serve me the bananas I gave you!'

At a loss, I suggest we go and eat out in the Rex neighbourhood. He turns down my offer:

'I didn't come here for that, nephew. I simply wanted to make sure you were all right, that you hadn't eaten stag or hind meat in all these years. I introduced you to your animal double, the fawn you saw in your dreams when you were only ten years old. That little creature is still out there in the bush, he'll live as long as you, or you'll live as long as he does…'

'Uncle, I know why you came: you want me to go and see my animal double in Louboulou.'

'No, no, it's too far, I don't suppose you've got the time with everything you've got to do in the few days you've got left here. Your double will understand, but you must give him something, I'll pass it on to him when I go down there next month…'

'Ah! I get it! How much?'

'Nephew, don't you disappoint me, I know you live in a country where money is everything, but believe me, it's not the only thing that matters in this world. The thing that has kept you alive this far is without price…'

'What can I give to an animal I've only seen once in a dream when I was ten?'

'Something that belongs to you, something of yourself…'

He digs in his pocket and takes out an empty test tube, the kind doctors use in hospital to take blood samples.

'Put your urine in there, I'll keep it in the freezer, then I'll go and pour it out by the stream in Louboulou where we were thirty-five years ago. The hind and the stag are gone now, your grandparents are dead, but their son, who's your age now, will still be there. He must smell your presence, your urine will be enough for him to continue to bless you…'

I go into the bathroom, and come back with the tube full.

This time he takes a bag out of his pocket and rolls the object up inside it.

'That's perfect, nephew, now I must be on my way...'

I hold out an envelope, with twenty thousand CFA francs inside.

'No, nephew, I didn't come to see you for that.'

'Uncle, please, take it, it'll pay for your trip back home...'

He hesitates for a few seconds, lowers his eyes, and pockets the envelope:

'Thank you, nephew.'

Last week

The suspended step of the stork

I write in a school exercise book, tearing out pages from time to time, for the slightest crossing out. As though the past were a straight line, like a wave, unmoving, unruffled by the wind's caprice. Sometimes, if I'm not happy with a paragraph, I dash into the kitchen and rummage in the little bin to find what I threw away yesterday. And I keep that instead, rejecting without a second thought words I was satisfied with only minutes before, and that seemed then to be a faithful transposition of my thoughts, images prompted by this return to the cradle.

A few 'budding writers', as they like to call themselves here, dropped in to see me at the request of the director of the French Institute, who merely said:

'They want to be writers, like any self-respecting Congolese, and they certainly have lots of manuscripts. I have never seen that in any other country I've worked in. Here, everyone is a poet! And they've been watching out for you for days! You must see them, and have a few words, it's important to them. There are over a dozen of them down there, I've organised a little place for them to sit. No one will disturb you there...'

We talked for over two hours in a corner of the lobby, just below my apartment. Some of them were fans of the poets

Tchicaya U'Tamsi and Maxime Ndebeka. Others of the novelists Henri Lopes, Sony Labou Tansi and Emmanuel Dongala. They read me their poems and waited for me to salute their genius, or tell them to revise what they'd written. They were somewhat disappointed when I suggested I had no such sovereign power.

Towards the end of these exchanges, during which each of them was trying to show his work to the others, to prove how much they deserved to be published – not counting those who had already paid to publish themselves, and who considered themselves above the others because they at least had printed proof of their status as writers – a young wordsmith asked me:

'Why do you write?'

I was beginning to feel rather tired, and said the first thing that came into my head:

'I don't know why I write, perhaps that's why I tear out pages I've already scribbled on, and throw them in the bin. I know I have no choice, I'll go and retrieve them the next morning and write them again. It doesn't matter how long it takes, as long as one day the book's finished.'

They laughed at that, but I didn't. Particularly since my bin right now is filled with crumpled pages…

I add it up in my head: I've come back to this town seventeen years after my mother's death, seven years after my father's and twenty-three years after I left for France. And yet the time has flashed by. I'm just a black stork, whose years of wandering now outnumber the years left to him to live. I have landed here, by the stream of my origins, one foot suspended, hoping I might stop the flow of my existence, whose smooth course is troubled by the myriad leaves blown down from the family tree.

I look for reasons to love this town, all smashed up though it is, and consumed by its anarchic growth. Like a long-lost lover, faithful as Ulysses' dog, it reaches out its long, shapeless arms to me, and day after day shows me how deep its wounds are, as though I could cauterise them with the wave of a magic wand.

This morning I open *Dark Side of the Sun*, a collection of poems by that most Pontenegrin of Congolese writers, Jean-Baptiste Tati-Loutard. I come across these lines, which exactly describe my present state of mind:

> *I trail in the wake of a tribe that is lost,*
> *A beast of the savannah plains, haunted*
> *By the rhythm of another herd…*

> *Seized by a longing to be outside of time*
> *To wander the obscure veins of the far-flung earth*
> *Where, relieved of a thousand earthly pains,*
> *The poor departed wander, long forgotten…*

I arrived like a migrating bird, its song half silenced, ready to accept the vast desolation of my country and to perch in the first tree with bark scuffed and scraped by the dry seasons. Perhaps I'm overstating, but the slightest silence troubles me, the least noise makes me jump, and inclines me to pull away from this inevitable encounter. I cast a candid eye on the places around me, and I know they look back at me in the same way, with big wide eyes. My shadow falls in front of me, as though showing me the way to go. Which should I trust, the shadow or the light? I see so many people shrouded in darkness, while all the time I've been away the sun has consumed the foundations of my childhood, and it is lost to me, ensnared in memories.

I hear a voice whisper that a child will be born long ago, its teeth already in place and thick fuzzy hair on its head. So I start to dig, with the stubborn persistence of an anthropologist. My tool? A pick corroded by the salt of regret. A pick whose handle is attached by the thin wire of memory. A stubborn voice tells me that behind all the mutations of the city of Pointe-Noire, a few remnants will still be reborn from the ashes. I've been digging up memories so long, the town now seems to me like the Catoblepas, the indolent monster in Flaubert's *Temptation of Saint Anthony*, which eventually devours its own feet. So I lend this erstwhile paradise my feet. I know if I keep on walking I'll find the places of my childhood. Because Pointe-Noire sleeps with one eye open, the one that weeps with a single, inexhaustible tear, a tributary of sorts, that flows on towards the Côte Sauvage.

I walk on through the streets of the city that's obsessed me for so long, bearing the weight of my ingratitude. Each stone is a fragment of the time when, clutching the braces on my school uniform, mouth open, fists clenched, I would run till I'd no breath left in me, and never thought that space might have its limits, that time went on flowing, even when I had my eyes wide open. It was at this time, I recall, that I'd watch the planes passing over the town bound for unknown destinations. What was in these huge, noisy birds that shook our wooden huts and frightened our house pets and babies? Each plane, I reckoned, must carry a piece of bad news. Very bad news. I crossed my fingers, hoping one of these birds of ill omen would never land on our town, that no one would come knocking at the door of one of our family saying:

'The doctor did everything he could, but sadly, God has called your relative home...'

Passages leading nowhere. Some streets still have no name. Others wander off, hoping to come out by the Atlantic Ocean, but creep round the back of run-down houses and wind up in blind alleys dotted with piles of rubbish, mountains that block the horizon.

A mangy dog slinks about with its tail between its legs, and looks at me out of the corner of its eye before running off. Must have thought I was a ghost. And I thought he was that dog from my childhood, Miguel. So we're quits…

Cinema Paradiso

There are no cinemas left in this town, not since the 1990s, when the spread of the evangelical churches hijacked most of the buildings dedicated to the seventh art. The Cinema Rex, once a mythical venue for the projection of films, became a Pentecostal church called 'The New Jerusalem', with pastors in their Sunday best heralding Apocalypses like there's no tomorrow, predicting the flames of Gehenna for wrongdoers, and miracles and good fortune for their flock. Disillusion is written on the faces of the blind, the deaf, the dumb and the lame. They loiter outside in the hope of divine healing.

Here, though, we would gather and wait every morning for the poster to be put up for the film to be shown in the early afternoon. Here we applauded the adventures of Bud Spencer and Terence Hill in *They Call Me Trinity* and *Trinity Is Still My Name* or *Super Fuzz*. The doorman, a professional boxer with a face like a gangster in a Wild West movie, called all the shots, telling us where to stand in the queue. He worked with his boxing gloves strung round his neck and at the first sign of unrest in the crowd he pulled them on. We were his subjects, who must yield to his will, comply with his whims, or we'd get an uppercut that would send us straight to the Adolphe-Sicé hospital. He would eject you from your seat if he felt like it, to make room for a member of his family, or someone who'd bribed him, and you just had to sit on the floor. He let children in to showings reserved for 'over 18s', in exchange for a hundred CFA franc coin. As far as I recall, he was the person responsible for most of the brawls that took place outside and inside the cinema, taking advantage of the venue to apply what he learned in the training gym. Since he was ugly, we promptly nicknamed him 'Joe Frazier', Muhammad Ali's most stubborn opponent.

With the arrival in the capital of the first martial arts films, our local Joe Frazier realised no one was scared of boxing now, because a fighter, unlike a karateka, couldn't fly into the air – what we called 'lift-off' – landing behind his opponent, and dealing him a fatal blow. We didn't realise these 'lift-offs' were just cinematic tricks, the actors were ordinary people like us. Overnight, posters of Bruce Lee in *The Way of the Dragon*, *Enter the Dragon* or *The Game of Death* replaced the ones of Clint Eastwood, Lee Van Cleef and Eli Wallach in *The Good, The Bad and The Ugly*. We lost interest in the spaghetti western actors, with their guns, which we could never own, and their horses, which we'd never seen up close. To us, karate seemed more accessible, you just had to learn the different katas and the philosophy of Master Gichin Funakoshi, the inventor of Shotokan Karate-Do. A number of dojos opened, where we handed over all our pocket money to Master Mabiala, who had proclaimed himself a black belt, 12th dan, and promised to reveal the secret of Bruce Lee's 'lift-off'. We all eagerly awaited the crucial moment when we would fly into the air, emitting a cry that would terrorise our opponent, but the so-called master dwelt instead on physical exercises that left us so exhausted that the number of pupils diminished every day. The truth was, we were his servants, he made us sweep out the dojo and his house, prepare his food, do the washing up or wash his clothes in the River Tchinouka. When people grew impatient and asked him when we were going to actually learn how to do the famous lift-off he would reply:

'You haven't finished learning all Master Funakoshi's katas yet, and even when you have, there'll be more katas, ones that were added by his disciples, in memory of him! So stop complaining, a bird can't fly the day it's born, its wings have to grow! It's the same with you, you have to allow the wings of your spirit to grow. One day you'll lift off without even realising!'

The brave souls who continued to take his classes did finally manage lift-off: Master Mabiala put them up on the roof of his house with the aid of a ladder, and told them to jump, while doing Bruce Lee's battle cry from *The Big Boss*…

Comedies did survive the breaking wave of the martial arts films, thanks to the energy and droll mannerisms of Louis de Funès in the saga of *The Gendarme of St Tropez* or in *Fantomas versus Scotland Yard* and *Fantomas Unleashed*. The French actor played the role of Commissioner Juve, who is obsessed with capturing Fantomas, public enemy number one. The anti-hero spends his whole time taunting Superintendent Juve, then melting into the crowd, to the applause of the cinema audience. It was one of the rare times we cheered a baddie; we would never do that in a spaghetti western, where everyone booed Clint Eastwood's enemies, demanding their money back. We particularly disliked it when villains Clint Eastwood had killed in a previous film appeared again in the next one. Since we took what happened in the cinema to be real, we were shocked and decided they must think we were too stupid to realise this was a piece of trickery designed to get us to hand over our money.

The Indian films escaped unscathed, thanks, no doubt, to

the interminable love stories that were their hallmark, as well as to the physical strength of the actor Dara Singh, not to mention the magical world of *The Magician from Hell*, and above all the music, which made us weep. We dreamed that we would one day go to India, where we would marry Indian girls, adorned with the same jewels as the actresses who adorned the screen. India was our Peru, the place where our dreams would come true, with a little bit of magic, learned from what we saw at the cinema. We would express ourselves with ease in Hindi or Urdu, since we already sang along in these languages with the actors from these countries, even if we didn't understand the words. Of course we'd be poor, but we wouldn't mind, because in these films the man with no money always ended up marrying the beautiful girl, beating the rich man to it. We would insist on kissing the women properly, none of that modesty we found so irritating, and which obliged you to work out for yourself that the main actor and his sweetheart must have finally slept together...

The projectionist at the Cinema Rex was a young womaniser who took a different girl up to his box at each showing. He picked them from among the young ladies who stood in line with us. In order to get chosen, they dressed up and put on lots of make-up, as though they were going to a party. We watched as they fluttered their eyes, to catch the attention of the technician, who took his time making up his mind. They'd bicker and insult each other over who would be the chosen one, privileged to watch the film through a little hole, right next to the one the images came through. Certain mishaps in the projection of the film were caused by the operator who, in order to impress the girl, explained all the tricks of the trade and what he called 'the enchantment of cinema'. Since he talked rather loudly, the spectators at the back could hear him explaining that a film had twenty-four images per second, and that a shutter closed off the light beam in between them to create an impression of fluid movement on the screen. Suddenly the young woman would get overexcited and ask to be allowed to replace the reels, and send out the images upside down, by mistake. You could hear them giggling, running off into their hidey-hole and starting to make out, to the applause of the crowd. We bore no grudge against the projectionist, since we knew the enchantment came from him and his skill in handling the 35mm projector.

The young man's work was not limited to what he did up in his box. You'd hear him hurtling down the stairs and dashing outside to receive the reels delivered from the Duo and the Roy, on the other side of town, in a little Renault 4L van. In fact we had to wait till the two other places had finished at least two reels of fifteen to twenty minutes each. This meant that for long films – like *The Savage Princess*, which lasted over two and a half hours – the courier had his work cut out, as did the projectionist, who got booed by the spectators if there was a delay and the showing got cut off in the middle of some thrilling piece of action because the van had broken down, or the other cinemas had had a hitch. Cool as a cucumber, the operator would simply show us an advert for Cadum soap, over and over again…

Outside the cinema a number of vendors spread their merchandise on the ground: comics featuring Tex Willer, Rodeo, Ombrax, Blek le Roc, Zembla, as well as the novels of Gérard de Villiers and San-Antonio. Sometimes you would come across an anthology of poems by Rimbaud, Baudelaire or the complete works of some author, published by Pléiade, bearing the stamp of the French Cultural Centre. Not something easy to sell, since in the 'bookshop on the ground' the most popular title was *African Blood* (volume 1, *The African*; and volume 2, *A Woman in Love*), by Guy des Cars. We were captivated by the two protagonists of *African Blood*, who were bound in a mixed marriage: a French woman, Yolande Hervieu – with her rich, racist ex-colonial parents – and the orphan from l'Oubangui-Chari, Jacques Yero, born into a poor family, adopted by whites who sent him to France to study in the 1950s, a time when the Negro was still struggling to prove to the world that he was a man like any other. The two protagonists would meet in the amphitheatre of the law faculty in Paris. We would hold our breath reading the passage where the white girl decides to introduce her black husband-to-be to her parents. We would be touched by the courage of the Frenchwoman, who would follow her husband to Africa, aginst the wishes of her parents, who were naturally opposed to their union. Throughout the first volume of *African Blood*, it was our own story we were reading, for the life of the couple on the black continent coincided with the independence of several francophone countries, and with l'Oubangui-Chari becoming the Central African Republic. The second volume showed us a couple in which the man had risen to a position of political power, arousing jealousy among blacks, as well as those whites who still liked to foster the view that their own race was superior. Later, when I arrived in France, I realised that Guy des Cars was an underrated author, so much so that his works were referred to as 'station bookshop novels', and the author sometimes nicknamed 'Guy des Gares'. But this in no way diminished my admiration for a man who, without a doubt, had inspired a whole generation of Pontenegrins, not to say French-speaking Africans, with a taste for reading.

The 'bookshops on the ground', which were often to be

found outside the Roy and the Duo, were dependent on the cinema clientele and therefore did not survive the demise of the cinemas. Times change; outside the Cinema Rex, traders have set up a makeshift telephone booth, offering calls for fifty CFA francs, selling mobiles and top-up cards. Others sell petrol in used pastis bottles they've collected in the centre of town. If the faithful of the New Jerusalem respect the spirit of the Bible, perhaps one day they will lay into these street traders, as Christ challenged the merchants in the Temple of Jerusalem.

It's early afternoon and I'm standing outside the building that delivered our dreams, bringing fictional heroes from all over the world to our neighbourhood. The Cinema Rex looks tiny to me now, though at the time it seemed vast, immeasurably so. Is that because I have since been to bigger cinemas in Europe and Los Angeles, or in India, where the cinemagoers actually become actors themselves?

I look at our old cinema, and can scarcely conceal my disappointment. A banner announces that a festival of Christian music will take place in the building. Two members of the congregation of the New Jerusalem, one tall, one small, are standing at the entrance, and give me a challenging look, as though they have guessed I'm planning on coming in. I approach the entrance and the taller one steps aside. Perhaps he thinks I have an appointment with the pastor. In the doorway I turn round and wave to my cousin Gilbert and my girlfriend, who are outside the Paysanat restaurant opposite. They cross the Avenue of Independence to join me.

At the sight of my girlfriend's camera, the little one frowns and rushes up to her:

'What's that, madame? This is a place of worship, no filming or photographs allowed!'

At once Gilbert comes to her rescue:

'My cousin's from Europe, he's a writer, he's writing a book about his childhood memories and…'

'Out of the question! Anyway, non-believers aren't allowed in here, writer or not!'

'Non-believer? You don't even know him, and you call him a non-believer?'

'I can tell by looking at him! If he was one of God's children he wouldn't turn up here with a video camera!'

'It isn't a video camera, it's just a camera…'

'Same thing!'

At a loss for arguments, my cousin decides to cut to the chase:

'Bollocks to your religion! Why do you film your Sunday masses, then, to get on TV, if God doesn't like images?'

The tall one intervenes:

'That's enough, now beat it!'

Furious, Gilbert pushes the little one aside and comes through to join me in the auditorium. My girlfriend does the same, while the two congregation members stand there like pillars of salt, shocked by our cheek. They come on through as well, and stick to us like glue. The tall one complains loudly while my girlfriend takes pictures:

'Stop filming in the house of God!'

A young man dressed up to the nines appears at the back of the worship area.

The little one growls like a cooped-up dog:

'Pastor, we couldn't stop them! We told them they mustn't enter the house of the Lord, but they came in anyway!'

In a calmer tone, the pastor asks us:

'Do you have the owner's permission to take photos in here?'

'Who is the owner?' my girlfriend asks.

'He lives just at the back, I don't think he's going to be too happy about what you're doing, you're violating private property. You'd better come with me and explain yourself. He will make you destroy the pictures you've already taken. It's not the first time this has happened!'

We exit in single file, the pastor at the front, and walk round to the back of the building. We find ourselves outside a plot where a man with a shaven head in a pair of bermuda shorts and vest is sitting in front of one of three doors in a long building up for rental.

The man notices us, opens his eyes wide in amazement when he sees me, and gives a great yell, leaving the pastor stunned:

'It's the American! I can't believe my eyes! You came to see old Koblavi!'

The pastor murmurs something in his ear, but Koblavi pushes him aside:

'No! No! No! He belongs here! He can photograph whatever he likes! You know the little street opposite the cinema, rue du Louboulou, that was his uncle who made that!'

The pastor stands with his arms drooping, his head on one side, and offers his apologies. Retracing his steps, he stops three times, to bow. Koblavi points to a chair at his side:

'Please, take a seat, little brother! Gilbert and madame, you go and film the cinema while I have a chat with my American…'

As soon as Gilbert and my girlfriend are gone, Koblavi assumes a pained expression:

'I've seen you so often on the TV, talking about your books.

I'm sorry, I'm ashamed, I've never read them… One day in an interview you even mentioned the Cinema Rex, I can't tell you what pleasure it gave me to hear that!…'

He looks up at the sky:

'The Lord has forsaken this town, and in doing so He also turned His back on the Cinema Rex… Sometimes I go into the auditorium, I close all the doors, and I sit down in the middle, just to remember the old days, when it was packed full. I can hear the noise, the shouting, I can still see the dreams of those young people floating up above their heads, forgetting their everyday troubles, just for an hour or two…'

'There are video recorders now, DVD machines, they can still have their dreams and…'

'That's all garbage, Mr American! How could that replace the atmosphere we had at the Cinema Rex? All these new things, it's the age of individualism! We've forgotten the true meaning of cinema, little brother! A film you watch at home doesn't affect you like a film you watch with a crowd at the cinema!'

He brushes away a couple of flies buzzing round his head and continues:

'You've come from America, let me recommend you watch *Becky Sharp*! Now that's real cinema, you take my word! And it's not just because I like Miriam Hopkins, though I have seen her before, in *Doctor Jekyll and Mr Hyde*! She's quite marvellous!'

He stands up, goes into the house, comes back a minute later with a photo of the American actress and hands it to me:

'Look at her, wasn't she beautiful? I insisted we show every film she'd ever been in at the Cinema Rex! Of course, people would rather watch shoot-outs and native Indians and Louis Funès fooling about, and all those idiot actors in the martial arts films. What can you learn from a martial arts film?'

He practically snatches the photo out of my hands and blows on it.

'I'm not having any dust on my idol's picture!'

He goes to put the photo back inside, and comes back with a bottle of beer and two glasses. I tell him about America, since he asks me. His eyes shine, he's almost like a child who's thrilled with a present:

'So you've actually seen Miriam Hopkins' two stars on the Hollywood Walk of Fame?'

'No, sadly, I haven't... I don't know that actress. I wasn't paying attention when I saw *Doctor Jekyll and Mr Hyde*...'

His face stiffens, as though I had just committed sacrilege. With eyes half closed, he murmurs:

'That's my dream, to go to Hollywood. I can't believe you live in the city of cinema and you've never found time to go and see Miriam Hopkins' two stars...'

Resigned now, he launches into a diatribe against the political authorities who failed to help him, obliging him to rent the Cinema Rex out to a religious congregation:

'Those politicians, they killed the cinema! And it's the same everywhere, little brother! Even in Brazzaville there are no cinemas left! How will young people ever get to know Miriam Hopkins? The cinema was something magical; wherever there was a picture house, the neighbourhood took its name. We've got the Rex district and the Duo district and the Roy district, but those politicians understand nothing about that kind of impact!'

Out of pure modesty, Koblavi avoids mentioning his historic and prestigious family name, the name of his Ghanaian grandparents, who, in the late 1940s, dominated the fishing trade in Pointe-Noire. But the thing their descendant is apparently most proud of is the cinema, whose demise he continues to bewail. He's almost apologising for having done a deal with these servants of God who sell tickets to paradise to their flock, unaware that many children in Pointe-Noire will never taste the atmosphere of those darkened movie houses, the succession of adverts and the opening credits of the film, followed by the applause of the audience. Noticing the little chain with a cross on around his neck, I say nothing critical about religion. But he touches it and tells me:

'Ah no, I don't belong to the New Jerusalem, I'm still a Catholic in the strict sense of the word...'

And finally he talks about my mother, whom he knew, about Uncle Albert, who was a friend of his father. As though speaking his last words, he murmurs very softly:

'I know my origins are Ghanaian, by my parents, but I've always felt Pontenegrin. D'you hear my accent? No one's more Pontenegrin than I am in this town! I've never been made to feel an outsider here, by anyone. This is where I live, this is where they'll bury me...'

Gilbert and my girlfriend are back now. They've spent over half an hour taking photos of the old Cinema Rex, and as they show them to Koblavi his features, sunk in nostalgia till now, light up with a smile. He even allows himself to be photographed, with his broadest smile:

'You should never look sad in a photograph, you don't know who might look at it in ten years' time, or twenty, or thirty, or forty, or fifty!'

He comes with us as far as the exit to his plot, and watches as we walk away.

We pass by the cinema again, where the two worshippers are still standing guard like a pair of Cerberuses. This time they don't dare look us straight in the eye. There's even a shadow behind them: the pastor, who watches us closely as we cross the Avenue of Independence...

Wild nights

Most districts in Pointe-Noire still have the same names, based on the activity of the inhabitants, or on their ethnic or geographical origins. The 'popo' villages, for example, all along the Côte Sauvage, were created by fishermen from Ghana and Togo, and by the popos from Benin, who came here in the late 1940s, like the Koblavi family. They had a monopoly on traditional sea fishing, using a technique, and material – the famous fourteen-metre popo pirogue, or dugout canoe – which the natives, coastal people of Vili origin, in their comparatively basic boats, which measured no more than five or six metres, could not compete with. The Senegalese, Malians and Mauritians, all of them great traders, made up the 'Grand Marché' district, where they put up the only mosque in a city which is otherwise mostly Christian or even animist. The boutiques selling imported pagnes, and the general food and white goods shops, were all kept by West Africans from these countries, who, as their own retirement drew near, passed the business on to their own compatriots, so that the Pontenegrins began to think they never died, especially as many of them shared the same surnames.

Was it a herding instinct which led those originating from certain departments in the west of the coutnry – the Niari and the Lékoumou – to come together again in districts such as

'Cocotier-du-Niari' and 'Pont-de-la-Lékoumou', while those from the south of the country, notably from the Bouenza department, and above all from the Mouyondzi region, settled in 'Pont de la Bouenza' district and 'Mouyondzi'? In this way the economic capital was in line with the rest of the country, where ethnicity was more important than nationhood. How could it have been otherwise when even at the pinnacle of the state, power was distributed according to this pattern? The southerners had felt frustrated for decades by the northerners' stranglehold on political power. Of course, from time to time the latter shuffled the pack and assigned the portfolio for hydro-carbons to a minister from the south. The population didn't fall for it: the minister was merely a stooge, whose only legitimacy came from the fact that he was from the southern region where petrol was to be found. This did not suffice to quash the south-erners' dissatisfaction. They were supposed to feel they had cornered the main source of wealth in the Congo, whereas in fact everyone knew the minister had no control whatsoever over the contracts, which all went to northerners.

Then there is the popular neighbourhood which the Ponte-negrins all call 'the Three-Hundreds', a name to be found on none of the various street signs. Is this a kind of delicacy or an attempt to wipe out the true story behind it? Tell someone you're from the Three Hundreds and their jaw will drop. You might as well live in a different town altogether, or on the raft of the Medusa. To avoid saying it, some people instead call it 'the Rex district', the name by which it is more officially known, thanks to the renown of the former cinema of the Koblavi family, but which hardly reflects the little kingdom of prostitu-tion dominated by itinerant girls from the former Zaire in the 1970s. These working girls were attracted by the superiority of the CFA franc at that time to the 'zaire', which was created on a whim as part of the policy of authenticity instigated by Mobutu Sese Seko. Sese Seko forbade his people to take Western names, and outlawed suits and ties in favour of the '*abacost*'.*

The girls weren't the only ones who crossed the River Congo, boarding the train at the station in Brazzaville to come and conquer Pointe-Noire, where the harbour activity guaranteed a stable economy. Builders, carpenters and rickshaw drivers arrived too, from 'the opposite country'. Since we speak the same language and have the same culture, the migrants felt quite at home, they melted into the crowd and would have gone unnoticed, had they not been prepared to do jobs which the Congolese turned down on the grounds that they were 'intellectuals'. The Zaireans who pitched up with us lived by the rule of 'article 15': 'Live as best you can' – a phrase dreamed up by a populace abandoned to their fate by the fourteen articles of the Zairean Constitution, cleverly stitched together by the kleptocrat Mobutu to keep himself in power for life.

The Three-Hundreds, situated behind the Rex cinema, was the area where the girls peddled their charms. This is still the case today. Housing made of wood or metal sheeting often stands side by side with unfinished – but inhabited – brick buildings. Should you lose your way in the winding streets of this sector, you will find yourself walking on condoms, which litter the ground. It's as though the girls desert their ill-lit alcoves after dark to come and work 'outside', as though, when it comes down to it, all cats really are grey.

*abacost: abbreviation of '*A bas le costume*', 'down with suits'. The Western jacket was perceived as a symbol of colonialisation. Mobutu, who was obsessed with 'Zaireanisation', imposed the *abacost*, a jacket worn next to the skin, between 1972 and 1990.

The name 'Three-Hundreds', according to some, refers to the war waged between the Zairean prostitutes and those from our town, who, way back when, had fixed the price of a trick at five hundred CFA cents. The Zaireans changed the rules by lowering the price to three hundred. A rumour went round the town that the Zaireans were more 'competent' and knew how to keep hold of their clientele, so much so that many men with wives and children were handing them most if not all of their salary. People had lost count of how many wives had come looking for their husbands in the Three-Hundreds. But how could you hope to find your man in this web of backstreets, passages, cul-de-sacs and dark dives, joining one plot to the next, one house to another, when he was probably fast asleep in the bed of some Amazon from the 'Other Congo'?

The battles between the sex professionals sometimes spilled out into the Avenue of Independence, where the two camps attacked each other with hammers, sometimes even throwing caustic soda in their adversaries' faces, a final solution designed to send them into retirement. We passed prostitutes with corroded faces who, even so, still continued to work in dark corners, where their features would be mostly hidden from the clients.

The public authorities became increasingly concerned by this situation. Probably because of certain practices said to be used by the Zaireans, particularly the use of gris-gris and poison with delayed effect, with the intention of wiping out their colleagues. And when sorcery and poisoning didn't work, they would engage crooks – usually compatriots – who were paid in kind to assassinate the Pontenegrin girls, and dump their bodies in the River Tchinouka, or on the Côte Sauvage. The ineffectiveness of the police, in addition to the prevailing mood of fear, led the Pontenegrins to abandon the territory in the short term, and move back towards the town centre. The result was a considerable loss of income, as the town centre, though busy during office hours, emptied after nightfall. They had no choice but to fall in line with the prices of the Zaireans, or shut up shop. The tariff of three hundred CFA francs eventually became the norm, and the two camps buried the hatchet. The only difference between them now was technique, and woe betide anyone who failed to take note of the words declaimed by Brassens in '*Le mauvais sujet repenti*':

> *There's an art to how you walk the streets,*
> *and how to shake your arse...*
> *Depending who you're out to catch,*
> *The chemist, the sexton, the clerk...*

When you walk alone in the Three-Hundreds district, the women watch you from their booths. They sense, just by looking, what brings the 'passer-by' to their fiefdom. There are men who hesitate, pretend they've lost their way, retrace their footsteps and then do exactly the same all over again a quarter of an hour later. The bravest walk confidently, putting up a smokescreen by whistling a happy tune; they never look behind them, and slip, swift as predators, into one of the lots, emerging only half an hour later.

Venturing this far myself, I don't know how the watching women will classify me. The fact remains that as I leave the Avenue of Independence, taking the first alleyway down to the heart of the district, I feel a presence behind me. I go past Koblavi's place, then turn around: a woman with legs like a wading bird's and brightly painted red lips comes towards me and shouts:

'What you looking for here? You a journalist?'

I start to walk faster, and try to reach the rue de Loukenéné, on my right. But the woman knows where all the little side roads in her neighbourhood come out, she cuts through the rue Moe-N'Dendé, and I find her standing in front of me again, determined, this time, with a piece of paper in her hands.

'I want you to read that, it's my story, I told it to another journalist, like you…'

Her prominent eyes have the look of someone who hasn't spoken in a long while, on whom life has weighed heavy for many years. She points to a plot a few steps away. Without hesitating, I go in with her, and in the yard find other women too, who all look me carefully up and down.

'I was the one who got them all to leave our native village and come here to work…'

Then, turning to the silent shadows, she exclaims:

'Don't be scared, girls, this gentleman is a journalist who works with the whites! I saw him yesterday near the Cinema Rex, and I promised myself I wouldn't let him leave without hearing my story. Then at last the whole world will know about our troubles. There's only one thing we want in this district: no sex without condoms!…'

The other girls all chorus:

'No sex without condoms!!!'

And in the lots behind us, like a rallying call they were waiting to hear, voices cry:

'No sex without condoms! No sex without condoms! No sex without condoms!'

I unfold the piece of paper the woman has handed me. It's a press release from the Syfia agency, dated 19 September 2009, entitled: *Congo-Brazzaville: Prostitutes care more for their lives than for money.* To this woman, this piece of paper is more important than her own birth certificate.

'Read that, monsieur, that's my story, and the story of all the women you see here!'

I smooth out the piece of paper and start to read out loud, with the woman nodding at every word:

Sex without condoms is a thing of the past. The sex workers of Pointe-Noire, Congo, now understand the dangers of their profession, in particular Aids, thanks to an organisation set up by a group of the women involved. These days they are intransigent with their clients, however much money he offers. This woman, who has asked not to be named, lives at present in the Rex district, in Pointe-Noire. A professional sex worker since 1990, she sees her clients at home, or rents a room. Her children live elsewhere, since 'they must be spared this ugly spectacle', she says. At 500 CFA francs (0.76 euros) a time, she earns over 80,000 CFA francs (122 euros) a month, enough to keep her family. She speaks about her profession without shame: 'Some of my family know. Life is a choice. You just have to make sure you stay safe when you work.'

While I'm noticing that the price of a trick is now fixed at five hundred CFA francs and that the district hasn't changed its name to reflect this, the prostitute points out:

'The woman who won't be named in this article is me. I'm not going to tell you my name either, we know what you journalists are like! You come here to get us to talk, and then when you go back to Europe what people read is the opposite of what we've told you, and of what you've seen! If you want to give me a name when you write the article, call me Madame Claude…'

'But madame, I'm not a journalist…'

'Yes you are! Why not be proud of your profession? Is it worse to be a journalist than a tart like me?'

'I'm actually here to retrace my childhood…'

'Oh, we've heard that before! That's like the clients who come by and make out they've got the wrong street and are only looking for directions! Bullshit! They want to get laid, but their conscience won't let them be! I know you're a journalist, I saw you with my own eyes yesterday, outside the Cinema Rex, with a man and a white woman, then you went and had a chat with old Koblavi in his lot, am I right?'

'Yes, but I…'

'Don't interrupt me, if you please! Did old Koblavi say bad things about us here in the Three-Hundreds?'

'No, not at all…'

Somewhat reassured, she hands me a stool and sits down herself on the ground. With a nod of the head she tells the other women to go, and one by one they leave the lot, without saying a word.

'I've nothing to offer you, Mr Journalist… Switch on the recorder on your phone, I'm going to tell you my story and please don't interrupt…'

I take my phone out of my pocket. She clears her throat, wipes the sweat running down from her brow with the back of her hand and folds her arms:

'I'm no little girl, Mr Journalist. I'm a woman who's lived, and let me tell you, this body you see here has been touched by filthy rickshaw pushers as well as the most high-up people in my old country, and yours too. This business is my life, it's what I know how to do best, and it's what has brought me here to this country. The day I can't do it any more, I'll pack my bags and return to my native land, way back to my village of Bandundu, where I'll work the soil. I told the other journalists I had children. It's not true, I made lots of things up, to shock people…

'I never had children, my seven brothers all left Kinshasa. Three of them live in Brussels in the Matongé district, and are married to white women; two of them manage to make a living in Angola, in the food trade, and the last two wander about the metro in Paris busking illegally, or so I've gathered from people back here on holiday. It's as if there's a wall between us, in their eyes I'm just the disgrace of the family. I never hear from any of them, perhaps because they resent me for following in the footsteps of our mother. Was it really her fault? I'm not judging, only God can judge our acts. Does anyone ever stop and wonder how a woman comes to sell her own body? Do they think it's an activity you choose like any other, like becoming a hairdresser, or a carpenter, or a journalist, like you? I studied at school, I even got my baccalaureate, but what use was it to me? A woman isn't born a tart, she becomes one. There comes a day, you look in the mirror, there's nowhere to go, you've got your back to the wall. So you cross the line, you offer your body to a passer-by, with an empty smile, because you have to seduce the client, like in any business. You tell yourself, you may debase your body tonight, but tomorrow you'll wash it clean, and restore its purity. So you wash it once, you wash it twice, but your scruples wear thin through habit, then you stop washing altogether, you accept your acts as your own, because no water on earth, including the Ganges, ever gave anyone back their purity. If it could, surely with all the streams and rivers and seas and oceans there are on earth, all men and women here below would be pure and innocent. I simply followed the destiny God saw fit to give me, even if all anyone sees in me is the pimp who controls the girls she's brought over from her own country. I'm the woman they throw the stone at, it's even written down in black and white in the Bible, I believe, but didn't Jesus protect tarts? I make a few of the men round here happy, at least that's something. My father had abandoned us when I was a child, and my mother brought me up to this trade, which she plied herself till the end of her days. Thanks to that we had a roof over our heads, my seven brothers and I. While the girls in our village were playing with their dolls, my mother was already explaining to me how to hold on to a man: cooking and sex, she said, the rest is an illusion, including beauty and diplomas. A beautiful woman with a diploma who can't cook and yawns in bed will soon find herself supplanted by an ugly ignoramus who can make a good dish of saka-saka and give her lover a great time in bed. I want you to put that in the article you write about us. I've never said any of what I've said to you to any journalist, but something makes me think you're different, you won't betray us, or old Koblavi wouldn't have invited you into his lot, I know him. But don't forget, call me Madame Claude... now, switch off your mobile, that's the end!'

I put my phone away. The women who had left the lot now came back, gradually, as though they had been listening behind the corrugated iron that defines the limits of the property.

I stand up and hold out my hand to Madame Claude. She keeps it a moment:

'Old Koblavi's a good man, he's never considered us tarts, he respects us. You mustn't say I said anything bad about him, you understand?'

'I understand...'

I look at my watch; it will soon be midday.

Leaving 'Madame Claude's' plot, I notice another group of

women opposite, watching me, wondering why I don't come over to them.

I head for the Avenue of Independence to look for a taxi.

War and peace

The taxi drops me outside Chez Gaspard. I almost turn back: it's a rough-and-ready restaurant in the Grand Marché district, and it's full and very noisy. A few customers have been waiting patiently for a while at the door. I'm surprised to see a guy sitting alone, thin as a rake, nod his head at me to come on over. Seeing me standing there, unmoving, undecided, he yells in a powerful voice:

'Come on! Be my guest!'

I go over to the stranger and sit down opposite him.

'I know you're thinking we don't know each other. But I know you! You're a writer, I've seen you sometimes on the TV! All these people sitting eating here are ignoramuses, they don't know who you are! But you're looking at someone who actually follows the news!'

'Maybe you were expecting someone who…'

'I belong here, I invite who I like. Two days ago I had lunch with a white journalist, yesterday with a colonel in the army, and this evening I'm with a writer! A word of advice: don't have the boar today, I've been told it's not fresh…'

He waves a hand in the direction of the waitress. She brings us two Primus beers and takes the tops off, her face expressionless, as though put out by the presence of this stranger. She goes back to the counter while my host eyes up her rear:

'I've got the file on that girl, and it's closed. She can sulk at me if she likes, I've already slept with her… Did you see the arse on her?'

I look round and nod.

'This country's changed, my writer friend…'

The stranger notices me looking at the scar that cuts his face in two, and touches it with his hand.

'Yes, I know, it comes from the war, the oil, I mean…'

He looks over at the customers sitting behind us, then at those sitting opposite us, to make sure they're not listening, then goes on:

'God gave us oil, even though we're only a little country with less than three million people. Why did he put all the oil in the south, instead of giving a bit to the north, so everyone would at least have a slice of the cake and we could stop fighting each other? But you know, I'm not complaining; when I think of some countries and the mess they're in and they don't have a single drop of oil, in the ground or out at sea!'

He raises his glass, empties it in one, and fills it again:

'Oil equals power! Where there's a war, there's oil. Otherwise, tell me this, why don't countries fight over water? Imagine a country without water, would its people survive? Oil has screwed everything up between the north and the south. And like the fuckwits we are, we've had a civil war over it!'

The waitress comes back to take our orders. I avoid the boar and go for the antelope with peanut butter. The stranger hesitates for a moment, then opts for the salted fish with mushrooms and glances again at the waitress's rear as she moves away:

'D'you see that? When I think I've had my leg over that and now she's playing up! Ah well, it was a bad idea anyway, the girl doesn't move in bed like she should, she makes you do all the hard work... what was I saying before that?'

'The civil war over oil...'

'Ah, yes, the war was all about getting control of the oil, to sell it in secret and buy villas in Europe! The oil here doesn't belong to the people, it belongs to the President of the Republic and his family. I won't name names because the walls here have ears like rabbits... The problem is that the president works with the French. The one who got overthrown didn't want to work with the French any more, he wanted to work with the Americans. So the French helped their friend, so he could stay in power, but the Americans didn't protect the new president, who was democratically elected. The Americans aren't stupid, they know they can go and make war somewhere else – in Iraq, for example – and get lots more oil than they would here. Why would they fight for a little country that has less oil than Iraq?'

Two women dressed in very short skirts enter the restaurant. High-heeled shoes. Heavy make-up. They walk across the room as if they're in some fashion show, and stop at the counter.

Suddenly the stranger addresses me as '*tu*', like an intimate friend.

'See that? They're on the prowl! They're tarts from the Three-Hundreds, but Pontenegrins, not from Zaire – those girls hardly ever come here! The war destroyed everything, now you have to do what you can to get by! What was I saying a minute ago?'

'The war, the French, the Americans...'

'Yes, we had a civil war here, you must know that, it was in the papers all over the world. The north of the country fighting the south. The northerners were in power, they didn't want to let go of the oil. I'm telling you, it was bad, the civil war. Weapons came in from everywhere. The northerners asked for help from the Angolans and the French, who came and invaded the south. The people in the south ran off into the bush to hide. We were dying of hunger, and from the mosquitoes, and other tropical illnesses. Some got eaten by crocodiles or lions. There was war on Earth and in Heaven too, believe me...'

He notices some of the customers are listening to us. He draws his chair closer to me and whispers:

'We saw military planes skim the tops of the forests. The people who ran off into the bush were called "refugees". The international community said we must help them, give them food, even if you can eat anything in the bush, like the Pygmies. But the Pygmies, they're a joke, I don't like them, they're too small and their stomachs don't get hungry every day like us big guys do, normal people, I mean. Pygmies are bastards who can go without eating or drinking for months on end, while people our size need to eat every day. Isn't that unfair? Who do they think they are, these Pygmies, going without food like that? And what do they do all day, hiding out there in the bush? They don't even know TV exists, that every single person has a mobile phone, and that for a long journey you take a train, or a plane! I don't like them at all, but you have to make do...'

The stranger's beginning to look a little weepy, as though on the verge of tears. He looks at the bottle for a moment, then continues:

'Mr Writer-man, you have no idea what went on in this God-awful country. It was dreadful! The newspapers didn't tell the truth, because the newspapers are written by – who? By spies, by which I mean, the French! When did the French ever tell the truth? They always lie! I saw the war with my own eyes, I was there, I was in the group of refugees. Sometimes the women gave birth in the bush because, between you and me, babies still get born even when there's oil and war in a country. The worst of it was, people went on making love even when people were falling like flies in the war. I expect you'll be wondering: why didn't they wait for the end of the war, to make love? Oh no, if you waited for the end of the war, people would forget how to make love, by the time the whole dirty war ended we'd be making love with animals! Nothing new there, though: throughout the history of the world, people have made love even in times of cholera…'

The waitress places our food on the table, just as my stomach starts to rumble. I'm hardly listening to my stranger now, just gobbling up my spicy dish, with my face just a few centimetres from my plate.

He peers after the two prostitutes who are just passing our table again:

'New girls, you can tell! The one with the lighter skin's not bad, eh? Look how she walks, like a freshwater fish!'

I don't react, and he suddenly adopts an affected voice, almost as though he's bragging:

'Oh, I was a refugee too, you know. Things got worse and worse for us, me and the rest of them, out in the bush. One day we heard three helicopters approaching. The rumour went round that they were from the international community. In fact they were helicopters from the French company that was extracting our oil. We thought they must be coming at last to get us out of this dreadful situation. So we came out of hiding like mice when they've just realised the cat who's been terrorising them actually has no claws and no teeth. We started shouting for joy. Dancing. Cheering. Kissing each other. We shouted: "Long live France! Long live France! Long live France!" Some people were so excited they shouted, like idiots: "Long live America!

Long live America! Long live America!" Perhaps because the Americans are the ones who liberate people. Even the French, didn't the Americans liberate them during the Second World War? Actually we didn't give a damn if it was the French or the Americans, we were just happy someone had come to liberate us. We thought: at last, we'll be able to make love in proper beds, children will get born on the maternity wards, not beside the river, as they have up till now. War is over! Long live peace! And the helicopters were coming towards us, like this…'

He imitates the flight of a helicopter with his arms, and the boss stares at us from behind the bar. My stranger realises this, and lowers his voice:

'Mr Writer-man, believe me, the helicopters were hovering right over our heads now, only a few metres away. We thought: they're going to throw us sacks of rice and sugar, bread and meat, which is what usually happens. We were all jostling to be first to lunge at the food. The oldest said we should let the women and children go first. And d'you know what happened? We saw the doors of the helicopters open, and it was the Angolans inside. Not the French! Not the Americans! The Angolans aimed their guns at us and opened fire, just like that! Even the birds were flying up in all directions, they couldn't work out what the hell was going on either! All you could hear was gunfire, every-where. People were falling, getting back on their feet, running, plunging into the river, sinking into the swamp. The soldiers chucked tear bombs at us, they mowed us down with machine guns. And the oldest among the refugees were shouting: "Take cover! It's an ambush!"'

The customers sitting behind us heard him shouting 'Take cover! It's an ambush!', but the stranger carried on regardless, caught up in his own tale:

'Oh yes, I was a lucky bastard, I was. I ran like the devil. I never once looked back. I went into a cave and stayed there for days, like in prehistoric times. The country was under the control of the president from the north, thanks to his Angolan allies. Which meant the war was over, since now the old president was back in power, having kicked out the one the people had elected. They told us to come out of our caves, because it was a time for national unity and the president from the north was there for the whole country, not just for the northerners. Gradually people began to leave the bush and return to their homes. When I got back home, my beard was so long it touched the floor. When I walked I looked like a zombie who had lost his way back to his tomb. I had almost totally lost my bearings, because there are no streets or avenues in the forest, like here. You can't say: "go straight on then take the next street you come to", oh no! In the forest you just go past trees, mountains and streams that could lead anywhere, and you sleep wherever you're sure there are no wild animals or Pygmy cannibals…'

Our neighbours at the table behind are more and more shocked. They've heard every word the man's said. They get up to leave. The war hero stops for a moment as though worried they might come and have it out with him, they might be northerners.

'Liar! Found another sucker to listen to you, have you?' one of them yells, shaking his fist at the stranger.

And turning to me, the same customer says:

'Monsieur, make sure this little mythomaniac pays for his own meal. He's like the fox in La Fontaine's fable: he lives off whoever listens to him! He's done it with others, he'll do it with you! He'll tell you he was a refugee, he was in the bush, but did anyone actually see him there? He's just a jerk, taking advantage of people who don't know him! He's never been in a civil war, except maybe in his own sick head!'

I expect the stranger to come back with an aggressive answer, but he just sits there, speechless, his chin sunk into his chest while the group walks past our table and out of the restaurant.

The stranger empties his glass straight off, then continues:

'Did you see the way that northerner talks to me, because I'm a southerner? So he thinks I wasn't in the war, does he? Great! And he thinks I can't pay my own bill? Honestly! I'm going to pay it, just to show you what hypocrites these northerners are, how they go round stirring up trouble! They're all the same! Just because they're in power, they expect us all to keep silent! Well, I won't be silenced, I will go on speaking the truth till the whole world knows what's going on in this country! They killed us, all us *lari* people, there was a genocide, everywhere around the region of Pool!'

Realising I haven't said a word up till now, he asks:

'Anyway, what are you doing here, in this country that's been ruined by the northerners?'

'Doing some book events, seeing my family, writing…'

'Hold on, hold on a minute, I should have asked you this first, because it really matters; are you from the north or the south?'

'Why does it matter?'

'OK, I'll put it differently; did President Sassou Nguesso pay your ticket and put you up here?'

'You said you wouldn't name names!'

'I don't care! Answer my question, Mr Writer: did Sassou invite you?'

'No, the French did, and…'

'Same thing! What you don't realise is, the president gave

money to the French, and they used the money to pay for your visit! I know everything! And I'm certain you're one of the Sassou clan!'

'I admire you for your certainty, but that's a pretty hasty assumption you're making there!'

'What do you mean, "hasty assumption"? I know everything! Were you in the war, then, like I was? Where were you when we were dying like cowboys? I was out there in the bush, and Sassou Nguesso was shooting at us with his Angolan and his French friends!'

He knows if he carries on like this I will get up and leave. He tones it down:

'I apologise, my dear writer, I do tend to fly off the handle, but that's all because of the war… What do I care, in the end, if you're from the north or the south? What I really wanted to tell you was, I eventually came out of the bush because the war was finished and the northerners were back in power. The country seemed calm again. We started to live again. We went to bars, to the sea, wherever. Bit by bit we forgot what had happened to us. Five years later, we finally had some elections, and the northern president, the one with support from the French and the Angolans, got licked! We jumped for joy. He practically got hounded out of the country and he went off to live in exile, in France. Now our leader's a southerner. And since he was angry with the French for supporting the northerner, he let the Americans exploit our oil. And the French didn't like that, because after all, they're our colonisers! So every day the French went to visit the ex-president from the north in his residence in Paris. They promised him they'd make sure he got back into power. But we couldn't see how a northerner could become president of our country again. Our country was crawling with

Americans. They tried to teach us to speak English, but that didn't work because the French passed on their terrible accent to us during colonial rule. We told the Americans they could do what they liked with our oil, we weren't going to learn their weird English, where you talk through your nose, like you've got flu. They didn't care, they signed contracts with the president from the south, and he signed away, and didn't realise he was actually selling them all the oil we already had, and any we might find in the future.'

Five people in military uniform come in and sit at the back. The stranger looks at them for a few seconds. He lowers his voice, knowing that if he talks loudly now we'll both end up in prison.

'Five years later we had new elections. The president from the south said he would stand a second time. But the ex-president from the north quickly came back from France to stand in the election too, with the support of the French. Unfortunately the elections never took place. The southern president claimed that the conditions for proceeding to the vote had not been met, and overran his mandate. The ex-president from the north said elections must be held. And that's how we got into a second civil war, which the president from the south lost, and that's how the northerners come to be back in power...'

I finished eating a while ago, and my head is buzzing with stories of civil war and my host's hate-filled abuse of his sworn enemies: the northerners. It's hard to get a word in, the stranger is so sure he knows everything, all conversation has to revolve entirely round him. My bottle of beer is still full.

'Aren't you drinking your beer?'

'I won't, thanks.'

He calls for the waitress and hands her the bottle.

'Keep it cold, I'll drink it myself tomorrow!'

He looks at his watch and exclaims:

'Time flies! I'm sorry, I have to go to a mass at La Source du Salut in the Fouks district. Do you want to come with me? That's where I pick girls up, at mass! You pretend to pray, and you go game-hunting while no one's looking! Come with me!'

'No thanks, I have to go and rest, I've got a busy day tomorrow, at my old lycée…'

He asks for the bill, and the waitress quickly brings it over. He fumbles in the inside pockets of his jacket, then of his trousers:

'Shit! My wallet! Someone's stolen my wallet! It's those northerners, they stole it!'

'But they came nowhere near us…'

'I know these northerners, they can rob you long distance! Listen, brother, can you pay today, and I'll buy you lunch later in the week?'

The waitress and the boss are standing behind the bar, and they snigger when they see me take out the money and place it on the table.

I leave the restaurant while the stranger, following behind, whispers:

'Come by tomorrow, I'll be here. Did you see those two prostitutes earlier? I'll book them for both of us. You can have the one with the lighter skin, I don't mind taking the dark one, it's OK. I'll pay, don't worry…'

Dead poets society

Towards the end of the morning I'm standing outside the lycée where I spent three years of secondary school from 1981 to 1984. Of the visits I had lined up during this stay, this one was underlined in red in my notebook, along with my mother's house and the Cinema Rex. Probably because in my mind there was an indissoluble link between these three places. I went to my mother's house several times, for the sake of my roots and members of my family. I wanted to see the Cinema Rex – or what remained of it – for the collective fantasy we experienced there, the roar of the crowd, which still resonates in me.

I pass through the gates to the lycée, hoping to relive the moment when my spirit ventured far from our native land, in search of universal knowledge, through world history, the geography of far-flung countries, the convoluted grammar of mathematics, the phenomena of the natural sciences and the exploration of the imagination via literature.

My heart feels weighed down by a surge of inconsolable apprehension, exactly the feeling I had all those years ago when I turned my back on *collège*, on short trousers and plastic sandals, and first set foot in this place, dressed in a beige shirt and trousers, the school uniform of the day, with proper town shoes which my mother had polished the night before, before explaining how I should walk to avoid wearing them out too soon, since they had to last the whole of this school year and, perhaps, into the next.

I remember how I felt, in this lycée, as though I had been parachuted into a different world, like a nervous little fledgling, lost among other species of flying creatures whose wings are already properly formed. I generally took shelter under the shade of the coconut trees in the quadrangle, while waiting for the bell to ring for the end of break.

In class, for the first few weeks, convinced that I wasn't as good as my classmates, I would go and sit at the back of the room, until one day the teacher of chemistry – a subject I dreaded – told me to go and sit in the front row because, he said, being tall, I could help him by holding up the test tubes to show the others when we were doing practical work. I had just turned sixteen and, unlike some other pupils of my age, who were starting to gang up on their parents, my own adolescent crisis expressed itself in a voice which whispered that lycée would prise me away from my family, because it was at lycée that they started to pick out the pupils who would leave one day, to go far from their country, never to return. This feeling was heightened by the presence of the Atlantic Ocean just behind the school campus, and the wind blowing in the coconut trees in the quadrangle. The constant presence of the sea, of Polish seamen with their crude tattoos, the Beninese fishermen, excited by a good catch, and the albatrosses startled by the height of the waves and the ships at anchor in the port with their worn-out sails gradually drew me away from the town. Deep down I dreamed of leaving, though I didn't know where, or how, or when. I wanted to be a loner in a crowd, invisible, when in fact I stood head and shoulders above my classmates, so that I got teased for having been kept behind a year, when in fact I was one of the youngest.

Sometimes, to get away from the gibes, I would go down to the seashore for an hour, before lessons, and wander along the shore, barefoot. After walking for a few minutes, I'd turn round and go back, trying to place my feet in the footprints I had left on the way. I knew that the pupils who came by later would panic at the idea that a sea monster, half man, half beast, was wandering about, with feet that had toes at front and back, to shake off anyone minded to track him. They would all run off screaming at the tops of their voices, while I sat there in my corner, stifling hysterical laughter...

Written over the highest building in the school campus is an inscription that surprises me: *Lycée Victor-Augagneur*. Even though my memories are muddled with the emotion of being back here twenty-eight years on, I'm still sure it wasn't called that back when I was here. So the town's very first lycée has reverted to the name it had in the 1950s, in honour of Jean-Victor Augagneur, a doctor by training, mayor and elected member for Lyon, then governor of Madagascar, who went on to occupy various ministerial posts in the Third French Republic, before being appointed governor general of French Equatorial Africa (FEA) in 1919. The name of this man, clearly visible on the main building, looks out over the Atlantic Ocean. How many passers-by notice it, and bother to ask themselves who this individual might have been? For many, the building has been here all their lives, maybe even with these capital letters cemented up high on its façade. I allow myself to wonder what lies behind the 'exhumation' of this French colonel whose name is presumably virtually unknown in his own country, whatever positions he may have held. Admittedly the city of Lyon paid him homage in the 1930s by calling a road not far from the general hospital, in the 3rd arrondissement, after him, but that wouldn't account for his name being as widely known as someone like Jules Ferry, that iconic figure in the creation of mandatory, secular state education, as well as an ardent defender of French colonisation.

Here he stands, and here he'll stay, Victor Augagneur, rescued from purgatory without fanfare or drum roll, by the people of Pointe-Noire. Here, as elsewhere in this country, the political authorities seem to believe that we can only reclaim our past – and thereby our dignity as a nation which has been independent since 15 August 1960 – by reinstating things from the past. Regardless of what their symbolic weight might be. Victor Augagneur has thus been added to the list of well-known French people who have survived the nationalist policy of our country. In Brazzaville we have, among others, la Case de Gaulle, and various streets named in honour of French soldiers and politicians: Jean Bart, François Joseph Amédée Lamy, Henri Moll, Félix Éboué, Jules Grévy, etc. The 'Marchand' stadium is dedicated to Jean-Baptiste Marchand, former officer of the Senegalese riflemen, head of the exploratory expedition known as 'Mission Congo-Nile', the aim of which was to reach the Nile ahead of the British and set up a new protectorate in the south of Egypt. The expedition failed when confronted with the over-whelming strength of the British army. And lastly, in Pointe-Noire, the Adolphe-Sicé hospital, where my cousin Bienvenüe is right now, owes its name to a military doctor, Marie Eugène Adolphe Sicé, a descendant of a governor of the colonies, and who, after having served in the colonial infantry, went to French

Equatorial Africa, where, from 1927, he was director of the Pasteur Institute in Brazzaville.

Entering the schoolyard, I spare a moment's thought for that most steadfast witness, Jean Makaya, our 'corridor supervisor'. He's departed this world now, the new general supervisor tells me, as he insists on giving me the guided tour of what now seems to me like a labyrinth. We go into his little office just off the main corridor, leading to the schoolyard. He talks about his predecessor, referring to him now and then as 'the late lamented', with an air of profound respect. He shows me a press cutting pinned up on the wall, signed by one Pépin Boulou:

'Do you remember Pépin Boulou?'

I hesitate for a moment, and pretend to be thinking. The general supervisor understands my awkwardness:

'But of course you do! He often talks to me about you. You were in the same class, in Building A, the literary section, and you both got your bac in literature and philosophy in 1984, I looked it up in the archives when they told me you'd be dropping in today. Ah well, Pépin wasn't lucky like you, he didn't get to go to France, he teaches here now. Some people had to stay behind, after all, for the torch to be passed on! It's a shame he's on holiday, he'd have been thrilled to see you again...'

I go up to the wall where the article in praise of Dipanda has been posted. I just skim the last paragraph, thinking that in funeral eulogies and tributes of this kind it's usually the last paragraph that really counts. I'm right, too, as it reads as follows:

1994 was the 40th anniversary of the Victor Augagneur

Lycée. This event passed completely unnoticed. What did not pass unnoticed, however, was the retirement of Jean Makaya, alias 'Dipanda'. A junior supervisor of legendary dynamism, he worked in this lycée from 1960 to 1994. Intransigent, quick to judge a face, hard working to a fault, he carried out his caretaking duties for thirty-four years, a loyal servant both of this lycée and the Congolese state in general. A veritable fossil in our school, the corridor supervisor, dubbed 'Dipanda', saw eleven directors come and go, and witnessed the graduation of most of the pupils, a familiar figure to all. Every single pupil could supply one or more colourful anecdotes about him. Born around 1939, his death passed almost unacknowledged in 1998; only four years after he took his retirement. On the 29th July 2002, on the initiative of the present director, Ferdinand Tsondabeka, a lively tribute was paid to him. Since then, Building A, traditionally reserved for the teaching of literature, has been named after him. As that august poet Victor Hugo wrote: 'in the quiet of his tomb he heard the world speak of him'. At a single stroke, indifference and neglect were set right once and for all.

I try to think of a 'colourful anecdote' connected with Dipanda, but none comes immediately to mind. A few snatches maybe, but they are so diffuse that all I can really remember all these years later is a man devoted to his duties, apparently ageless, who loomed over us with a stick in his right hand, which he was happy to use if he thought a pupil was showing disrespect. I can still see him standing outside the gates, checking that our school uniform was clean, properly ironed, and that certain young rascals weren't fooling about, turning up their collar, or rolling up their sleeves to expose their biceps, as was the habit of some young 'louts' from the rough neighbourhoods. At the beginning of each school year, Dipanda brought all the new pupils together in the schoolyard and lectured them for an hour on how lucky they were to be taking their place on the benches of this noble institution:

'This lycée is a snapshot of the history of this town. Of the whole country, even, the whole of Africa!'

He would then reel off all the names of significant former pupils: prime ministers, army generals, directors of large companies. Not omitting to mention that it was in 1963 that the first female teacher in the Congo, Aimée Mambou Gnali, gave her first lessons:

'Madame Gnali – what a woman! She arrived three years after I was made supervisor! I helped her a lot, young boys can be dreadful with women!'

Dipanda's view was like that of many of those sentimental-ists who looked upon the Lycée Victor Augagneur of the 1950s as the 'Lycée Louis-le-Grand' of the tropics. They would refer to the area around the school as the 'Latin Quarter' of the Congo, underlining the extent to which the institution stood for rigour and scrupulousness – in short, was a school where merit alone separated the wheat from the chaff.

We chose to distance ourselves from this rather over-insistent adoration, especially since it came mostly from those who in reality were nostalgic for the colonial school and viewed every-thing through the prism of the past. So, if a classroom fell into disrepair, you would hear them complaining in the corridors, out of earshot of the principal, Pierre Justin Makosso:

'It's all because the blacks are running the lycée now! If the whites were still here they'd have repaired the roof and repainted the walls!'

According to them, Victor Augagneur had been the best school in the world, before the modern era came along and changed everything for the worse. They claimed that the primary school certificate back then was equivalent to the baccalaureate in our day, and the baccalaureate under colonial rule had been easily equivalent to three years' study at the Marien-Ngouabi University in Brazzaville. There was a general attitude of resignation, which encouraged the previously colonised to imagine that the Negro was essentially lazy, chaotic, careless, and that these shortcomings had undermined the Western way of doing things, which had been guiding our future nations in the right direction.

In their nostalgia they seemed to have forgotten that it was that great colonist Victor Augagneur who, after his promotion to the leadership of French Equatorial Africa, imposed the press-ganging of all able-bodied men living along the construction route of the Congo–Ocean railway line. Over twenty thousand people lost their lives in the gruesome construction of this line, and many more were left mutilated and maimed. One vestige of that peril is a landmark familiar to all Pontenegrins: the station in Pointe-Noire, dreamed up by French architect Jean Philippot, who also designed the station at Deauville, hence the apparent resemblance some have observed between the two buildings.

It would be no exaggeration to say that Victor Augagneur was one of the promoters of a modern form of slavery, which drove people from all over the Congo to leave their land and hide in the bush, to escape what amounted to certain death. Victor Augagneur employed all the means at his disposal to achieve his cherished goal; to make Pointe-Noire into the terminus of the Congo–Ocean network, and hub of the whole of the Middle

Congo, of which it would become the capital – thus avoiding any dependence on the part of the French colonial administration on the transport network of the Belgian Congo, with its railway line connecting Matadi to Leopoldville.

In his own lifetime, Victor Augagneur was not privileged to see his name carved atop the main building of the Pontenegrin lycée. The lycée was inaugurated in 1954, two decades after his death. Initially it was called the 'Classical and Modern Secondary School'. People noticed it didn't have a real name, and an adjustment was made: 'Classical and Modern Secondary School Victor Augagneur'. Some people found this a bit excessive. In the end they opted for the more straightforward version: 'Lycée Victor Augagneur'.

However, the constant changing of titles wasn't over yet, and Governor Victor Augagneur's place in posterity was by no means yet secure in the coastal city. The Marxist-Leninist regime of the 'Immortal' Marien Ngouabi, who came to power in 1968, would upset things all over again. Indeed, during his reign, there was much talk of 'independence of spirit' and solidarity with communist brothers the world over, how the proletariat of all countries must unite for the final struggle. Above all, 'mental colonisation' must be wiped out, and the order went out for the systematic clean-up of anything which recalled, dimly or vividly, the domination of the white man, and above all of the new enemy, capitalism and its ideology of exploitation of man by his fellow man. The policy must start at the top, so under Marien Ngouabi the country would be called, not the Republic of Congo, but the 'People's Republic of Congo'. Schools, roads, railway stations with colonial names were all gradually rebaptised with the names of Congolese heroes or promoters of communism. The secondary school where I had recently passed my school certificate, or 'brevet', was called the Trois Glorieuses secondary school in memory of the three days – 13, 14, 15 August 1963 – during which the Congolese trade unionists and their sympathisers ousted Fulbert Youlou, a polygamous priest of the Roman Catholic church, and first president of our country, who tried to impose a one-party state.

By the time I passed into the second year of lycée in 1981, the school had already changed its name and had been known as the Lycée Karl Marx since 1975. President Marien Ngouabi had been assassinated by his own supporters in 1977, but the politicians who succeeded him pursued exactly the same line of 'scientific socialism', mixed up with a little tropical capitalism. We looked to the Soviets to teach us mathematics, chemistry, physics and philosophy. Obviously we now swore by Lenin, Engels and Marx; all those other philosophers, like Plato, Kant and Hegel were too idealistic, according to our authorities, and were outlawed, to be mentioned only in contrast to the 'true' philosophers, those who had introduced and analysed 'historical materialism' and 'dialectics', notably the authors of the *Communist Party Manifesto*, whose portraits hung proudly in every classroom, on the main streets, at intersections, beside the official photo of the man who was president of the republic, head of the government and president of the central committee of the single party, the Congolese Workers' Party, all rolled into one. The systematic linking of our head of state with Karl Marx and Engels led us to feel that all three were thinkers of equal stature, even if we only ever learned speeches by our president, rather than profound philosophical texts. For the average Congolese person, the president was as much of a philosopher as Marx or Engels. So you could study Marxist-Leninist thought in the speeches of the head of state, instead of wasting your energy reading a great tome like *Das Kapital* by Marx, or a short but nonetheless deep book like *Ludwig Feuerbach and the End of Classical German Philosophy*, by Engels. So the pupils mostly quoted the president, who himself had quoted Marx and Engels, and thus we learned what some secretly termed 'the philosophy of poverty'.

One direct consequence of the influence of the Soviet Union on our education was the decline of two languages considered to be the languages of the capitalists, and therefore to be banned: English and Spanish. You have to wonder why we continued to use French, with the implication that this language hadn't come from the capitalist world, and was actually a Congolese language.

The fact remains that Russian became the first foreign language, particularly since the USSR offered the Congolese bursaries by the bucketful, despite the shortage of candidates who, for the most part, secretly dreamed of going to study in France, rather than of joining the ranks of cut-price graduates returning from Moscow, who were then given jobs at the School of the Party, to spread Marxist-Leninist ideology. In an attempt to get the pupils to look to the Soviet Union, some teachers who were members of the Congolese Workers' Party would sneer:

'What the hell use is English going to be to you, since you're never going to go to England?'

The supervisor isn't surprised when I ask to meet my old philosophy teacher, who is by far the teacher who left the greatest impression on the 'Stream A' pupils in my generation at the lycée. Since we didn't know his first name, we called him 'Monsieur Nimbounou', or behind his back by his nickname, 'Nimble'. We'd pass him on the Avenue of Independence, standing at a bus shelter, with his briefcase, on to which he had stuck a picture of Auguste Rodin's *The Thinker*. When asked what it symbolised, he would reply:

'Throughout our lives we should be constantly challenged by the thoughts of the great writers. Rodin's *Thinker* is an example of the man who is constantly engaged in thought, and having him with me imposes a spiritual discipline which even religion cannot offer the faithful...'

The supervisor tells me that Nimble doesn't teach philosophy any more, that he is a Board Inspector now. And he's over in a different part of the building where a teachers' meeting is being held.

We cross the schoolyard and go over to the meeting room. Outside, the supervisor hesitates, asks me to wait for a moment, and goes in without knocking. Less than two minutes later he comes back out, followed by a man in a suit.

For a moment I don't move, transfixed once more, I think, by the fascination this teacher exerted on us as pupils, when he arrived in class with his briefcase, and suddenly all the chatter ceased. He would enter slowly, place his things on a table and sit down on a chair by the window. He would open a book and begin the lesson, without a hint of a cough in the room. His teaching was seen as an invitation to independent thought, a far cry from the slogans of the Party. Setting aside Karl Marx and Engels, he would randomly invoke Descartes, Montesquieu, Voltaire, Plato, Kant and Nietzsche. Philosophy seemed to us like an extraordinary odyssey, spiced up with entertaining anecdotes, such as the one about Diogenes of Sinope who lived in a tub. Monsieur Nimbounou took a sly pleasure in explaining to us how this particular philosopher was a sworn opponent of conformism, barking like a dog, pissing and masturbating in public. And when he spoke of Epicurus and the cult of pleasure, we all smiled, and he did too, with that sly look of his, which he has to this day. He would stand up, looking very serious, and say:

'Now Epicurus had the right idea, he defined pleasure as the absence of pain. I share his view myself, though it must be said that the perversity of human beings is such that sometimes pleasure, for some people, can only be achieved through pain. Which goes to show that at all times you must seek the antithesis of any given thesis, and from there proceed to a synthesis which reflects your independence of mind...'

Hypnotised by the breadth of his knowledge, we created a discussion group in the lycée. During these sessions, in which we also talked of poetry, we would imitate him by reading whole pages of some 'capitalist' philosophy which was taught nowhere except in our class. We were disappointed to discover that the study of historical materialism did not provide the same delight or enthusiasm as classical philosophy. But Monsieur Nimbounou could not entirely neglect the programme imposed by the Ministry of Education. So he would skim over the thought of Marx and Engels and quickly come back to what he considered true philosophy, that of the school of Antiquity.

We have been chatting for ten minutes or so, not far from the meeting room. Monsieur Nimbounou is talking about my books, some of which he has read:

'My favourite of all is *Memoirs of a Porcupine*. Perhaps because, without realising it, you posed some philosophical questions in it. Can animals be philosophers? Isn't philosophy exclusively a feature of human thought? That's pretty well what I taught you back then...'

The supervisor agrees with a nod of the head, while, to change the subject, I tell Nimble that I thought he had retired.

He smiles:

'Our country doesn't yet have enough philosophers for me to be able to retire. And I'm afraid that until my dying day there will be some who go on believing it's possible to live without philosophising…'

Just as I'm leaving him, I take an envelope from my pocket and hand it to him. He smiles again and pockets it. In the meeting room a voice can be heard saying:

'What about us? Don't we get anything?'

Nimble turns round, surprising some of his colleagues, who are watching through the slats in the blinds.

'He wasn't your pupil, that's the difference,' he says, in their direction.

He folds me in his arms and murmurs:

'I have to go back into the meeting. I'm so glad you came… Don't forget: some philosophers only interpreted the world; what we have to do now is transform it. That's possibly the only thing I learned from Engels, for everything else you're better off with the philosophy of Antiquity…'

He returns to the meeting room while we go back the way we came and the supervisor asks me quietly:

'What was in the envelope?'

'Just some money, to buy a beer.'

'He doesn't drink…'

'Well, he can buy himself a lemonade, at least…'

At the exit to the lycée the supervisor looks sad:

'You will come back and visit us again one day, won't you?'

'Of course!'

'But when? Twenty-eight years from now? We'll all be dead,

and maybe the school won't even be called Victor-Augagneur any more! I'll have gone to join our dear departed Dipanda, up above...'

I reply, without conviction:

'I'll try not to leave it another twenty-eight years...'

Jaws

Few Pontenegrins ever dare come as far as this part of the port. Placide Mouembe, my childhood friend, has driven me here, at my request. But he prefers to remain at a distance.

'Don't go any farther!' he yells, increasingly anxious as I gradually advance towards the water.

In his car, all the way here, he kept telling me I must be careful. And he gave me strict orders:

'We can go the whole length of the port and back, if you want, but please let's not go to that cursed place where there are all those rocks. Strange things happen down there. I don't want anything to happen to us...'

I decided he must be thinking of the times we used to roam down the beach in the hope of finding a wrap left behind by a mermaid, the famous Mami Watta. According to legend, whoever found it would become very rich. The Pontenegrins back then thought that the very wealthy people in our town must have happened upon the wrap of the woman with the fishtail and long golden hair. People from the rougher parts of town would be up at dawn to dash to the bit of the wharf where she was said to live. The most gullible among them would describe the features of this aquatic being with great attention to detail, as though they had actually seen her. She was blonde, or maybe she was black, or maybe a woman with porcelain skin. She was huge, surging out of a great gaping abyss far out to sea, and would come and lie down to rest a few centimetres from the wharf when the ships had gone out. Her piercing eyes lit up the whole of the Côte Sauvage as she stretched out on the sand to comb her hair. What time did you have to get up, if you wanted to see her? Some said around midnight, or even two in the morning. Others said around four. And even so, no one dared come here at these times.

But no, Placide wasn't referring to Mama Watti, but to a different mystery:

'The ocean keeps many things in its belly... the sea is dangerous still, brother, and has no pity. Do you know why the water is salty?'

'I've already heard that one...'

'Yes, the sea tastes salty from the tears of our ancestors, who wept as they made their cursed passage during the slave trade.'

Once we were through the entrance to the port and had parked the car, he began to look worried:

'It's a bad day to be down by the sea. There's hardly anyone here, the boats look like ghosts watching us, ready to shove us in the water. I'm not going near those rocks...'

I was so insistent, though, that finally he gave in:

'All right, then, let's go, but we mustn't get too close!'

All around me are the rocks where the waves come to die. As I approach, the sea suddenly falls calm. I can't see what Placide is frightened of, it's such a peaceful place, where any tourist would dream of spending an entire afternoon.

I turn around: Placide is waving at me to come back, but I

don't move, I look out across the stretch of sea and imagine what might be lurking in its depths.

A cormorant lands not far away; I turn my head to look at him just as a gigantic wave comes out of nowhere and smashes on to the rocks, wetting my trousers. From a distance, another, even bigger one races in at breakneck speed. I retreat and run back to join my friend, whose face is rigid with terror:

'What did I tell you? Did you see that? Wasn't that weird, those two waves? This part of the sea is the kingdom of darkness, it has teeth here and anyone who intrudes on her peace and quiet will be crushed! This is where the bodies of the drowned are washed up. Wherever you happen to die in these waters, it's here that your body will be found! All the sorcerers in this town come and do their stuff here, that's why I didn't want us to get too close to this Zone of Death. The water looks peaceful enough, but if someone comes to stand on the rocks it turns rough, and swallows him with the third wave, which can be as high as a building with five or six storeys, believe me!…'

The cormorant I saw earlier passes overhead. Placide follows his flight and concludes, chillingly:

'Those birds work hand in hand with the spirits of the sea. They're accomplices, they tell the monsters of the sea if someone's here! The bird that's just flown over is disappointed, because he didn't get what he wanted: you! Listen, let's go back, we're better off having a drink down by the Rex…'

That evening, after a drink at the Paysanat, Placide dropped me outside the French Institute. I couldn't sleep. I kept thinking of the two waves, and wondering what would have happened at the third wave, if I had stayed on the rocks…

I don't remember ever having bathed on the Côte Sauvage as a teenager. I only ever went down there with the other kids in the hope of getting some sardines, jack mackerels or sole from the Beninese fishermen to take back to my mother, in exchange for help unloading the Ghanaian pirogues. We also went with the secret hope of spying on the half-naked women, particularly white women. The grown-ups said they didn't know how to hide their 'nether lands' and made a great exhibition of themselves applying their suncream. Our curiosity bordered on obsession, since we were determined to check whether the blondes also had blond pubic hairs, and if the redheads were red 'down there' as well. Grown-ups idolised body hair to the point where you'd hear them whispering: 'I chatted up this girl today, wow, she's beautiful! She's got hair everywhere, long and shiny, straight hair!'

Obviously, because these women depilated their bodies before they went into the sun, you had to get really close to see anything. Startled by our invasion, they would call us all the names under the sun, and go and complain to the coastguard of the Côte Sauvage, who would throw us off the beach.

Many of us, like myself, had never bathed in the sea here, scrupulously following the recommendations of the local sorcerers as to how to keep hold of our physical strength. We often went to ask their advice, and they would prepare gris-gris for us, to make us invincible when we got into fights. With the gris-gris to protect you, if you gave your opponent a thump on the head, he would fall unconscious, or his head would go into such a spin he'd start picking up the garbage that lay round about him. People said that some of these gris-gris, made in the most far-flung villages in the south of the country, like Mayalama, Mpangala or Boko, were so powerful that if you slapped a tree, the unripe fruits would fall and the leaves would turn to dust. Most of the kids were tempted by these fetishes from the age of fourteen. You just had to turn up at the sorcerer's house with one litre of palm wine, and one of palm oil, a packet of Gillette blades, some cola nuts, chillis and charcoal. The guru would get out his arsenal of amulets, murmur a few obscure words, light some candles and ask you to hold out your wrists. He'd grab a Gillette blade and make three little cuts on each of your wrists. Once the blood began to flow he would rub on a black powder, which stung. You were not allowed to cry out or give any sign that the power was entering into you. For the pain he'd get you to chew on some cola nuts and drink a glass of palm wine. You paid him for his work, and he gave you a list of things you mustn't do: don't look under your bed, don't put your left foot down first when you get out of bed, don't approach women, and most of all, don't swim on the Côte Sauvage. How could you check that the power had entered you? The sorcerer would slap you several times. After a moment, you went into a trance, mind and body. Then he'd hand you an empty bottle and ask you to smash it over your own head. If the glass broke without cutting you, it was a total success. Then you had to go and pick a fight with someone in the street, to be quite sure you were as strong as Zembla, Tarzan and Blek the Rock, all rolled into one...

Indeed, the Côte Sauvage has always been the object of darkest speculation on the part of the Pontenegrins. In their minds, the sea was where the sorcerers from all over town met to draw up a list of all the people who would die in the coming year. Accordingly, any death that occurred here was considered a mystery, the key to which was closely guarded down at the very bottom of the ocean, where all the evil spirits lived, disguised as the fauna of the deep, feeding on human flesh. In short, as soon as a body was seen floating on the ocean surface, these creatures reached out with their giant octopus tentacles to catch them and drag them down to the ocean bed, devouring them at their leisure.

In the 'news in brief' column of our local newspapers back then, they kept a record of drownings which eventually turned out to have been sacrificial deaths, sometimes instigated by the family of the deceased. Many of those who drowned were albinos. Local people believed albinos possessed supernatural powers and that if, for example, you slept with an albino girl, you would recover your virility, or get rich. Such was the prejudice against albinos, the sacrificers tended to overlook the fact that albinism is not a curse, simply a hereditary illness found not only among humans but among certain animals too, such as amphibians and reptiles. From an early age we were indoctrinated with this harsh social reality, and we went along with it, so that if we encountered an albino we already began to imagine them drowned, their corpse, at best, washed up on a beach, if the underwater creatures were already busy devouring their previous victims. Charlatans of all kinds stepped into this breach, decreeing that true attonement could be achieved only by sacrificing those individuals whose skin was sufficiently pale and eyes colourless, red, light blue, orange or purplish-blue for them to be blamed for the entire community's woes. The justification was almost always the same: albinos had not been born like that by chance, they were whites gone wrong who unfortunately had landed here, and in any case, once thrown into the sea they would return to Europe where they would recover the true colour of their skin. The sea was the perfect setting for the drama of this return to the cradle. That was the whole point – white men had arrived at our shores by sea, to capture the Negroes and carry them away, to a place no one ever returned from – except albinos, who came back with this strange coloured skin. So we were doing them a favour, sending them back to Europe.

What with all this, we were not exactly surprised that no albino kids ever came to walk with us along the Côte Sauvage. Their parents, if they really cared about their children, would keep them locked up at home, since even out in the street they were not safe from stone-throwing, not to mention the dogs who joined in too, barking at them as though face to face with a monster.

The Côte Sauvage had also swallowed up another category of individuals, dropped unscrupulously into its waters: the crippled and lame. It was a pretty sordid image when, the day after an act of this kind, the sea held on to the corpse of the deceased, but returned their wheelchair. Someone would recover it and take it to sell in one of the markets downtown, where no one would ever question the provenance of this damaged merchandise. There were so many disabled folk dragging themselves around the town, the seller usually found a buyer within the hour.

The painting

Walking up the Avenue Général de Gaulle, in the town centre, you come to the Kassai round-about and memorial, bearing a commemorative plaque with the eloquent inscription:

To the Free French of the Middle Congo, who joined forces to free the Mother Country under the insignia of the Cross of Lorraine. 18 June 1940–28 August 1940 …

Pointe-Noire jealously preserves its past as a colonial town, and the roundabout recalls the demarcation line between what was once 'white city', on one side, and the 'native quarters' on the other. In those days native inhabitants would leave their insalubrious shacks first thing in the morning and go into the 'white town' to sell their labour as gardeners, kitchen hands, boys, etc. Of all francophone African writers, it is probably the Cameroonian novelist Eza Boto (Mongo Beti) who best describes a colonial town. In his novel *Cruel City*, the northern part of the city of Tanga is a 'little France', imported into the tropics, with its sumptuous buildings, its streets in bloom, while the southern part rots in extreme poverty, without electricity and, when the town sleeps, terror is spread through the streets by criminal gangs.

Downtown Pointe-Noire is in this sense a kind of French territory, as the commemorative plaque at the Kassai roundabout seems to suggest. Unsurprisingly, just a stone's throw away, is the French Cultural Centre – now known as the 'French Institute of the Congo, Pointe-Noire', to the irritation of the Pontenegrins, who wonder why this title is any better than the old one, which is fixed in people's memories.

It's a two-storey building, with four apartments on the first floor: the director's and three others for international charity workers, writers and artists invited by the Institute. For the past ten days I have been staying in one myself, and I will be leaving the day after tomorrow. Several works by Congolese artists hang on the living-room walls. I look, in vain, for the names of these artists, whose talent will probably never be known to the public. One painting in particular intrigues me: it shows a young woman, whose blank stare introduces a note of sadness into the room. When I arrived I thought I might move her, then I kept putting it off to the next day, perhaps out of laziness, or perhaps because of the secret power of the subject, who, I somehow felt, would not appreciate the gesture. To avoid her stare, I stopped turning my head to the right when I sat in the chair to write. Sometimes I turned my back to her, but that never lasted long; a voice whispered to me that the woman was reading over my shoulder and was responsible for most of my crossings-out. As though she objected to my daily writing-up of the past, though she knew nothing about my childhood and I must have been older than her, despite the age assigned to her by her creator, catapulting her into the past. With only two days left here, moving her would bring me more qualms than relief. She was there before, she will still be there, and I am only passing through. The director of the Institute, Eric Miclet, has assured me that he found her in this position when he took over his duties, and that his own inclination was, if something blends into the background, let it be. Teasingly, he said:

'She's a bit like the guardian of the apartment! She's seen everything, heard everything, for years now. But she's never once, in all that time, told tales on the guests who've stayed here.'

As soon as the door opens, the woman frowns and seems to resent the light. So until now I have been sure to close the door quickly behind me, to preserve for her the image she likes to give of herself: a woman alone, with an expression of gloom pulling lines around her lips and eyes.

The background of the painting is incomplete, some of the birds have no wings, and the sky is only vaguely sketched in. Occasionally it makes me think of the film *The Painting* by Jean-François Laguionie, in which a painter leaves a picture unfinished, and you see a castle, gardens and a strange forest. There are three categories of people in the work: the Allduns – completely painted – the Halfies – still with some things missing – and the Sketchies, who are only vaguely there. The Allduns hunt down the Halfies and take the Sketchies into captivity. The only person who can establish peace between the protagonists is the Painter himself. Ramo, Lola and Plume set off to look for the artist, so he can come back and finish the painting…

I have no wish to track down the painter of this Congolese picture. I will settle for what Eric Miclet told me: if something blends into the background, let it be…

House of stories

Each time I go up the stairs in the Institute I remember how I used to climb them when I was only twelve years old, and there was nothing up there but books and readers from the remotest districts of Pointe-Noire. Since that time there's been a lot of building work, and I still can't find my way around. The old theatre has gone, and a new performance area has been created at the rear of the building. Young people arrive in the morning at the cyberspace in the basement, and don't leave again until closing time.

This used to be the only library in the whole town, with a children's books section which we made great use of. I'd put myself in a corner, near the window, and lose myself in comic strips whose heroes were trapped in this room, unable to leave and have new adventures because we wouldn't let them out, for fear they'd go and bewitch other children, in a different country. For us they were living people, of flesh and blood. We entered the premises with the sense that we were leaving Pointe-Noire for a long journey through a fantasy world where we were held captive. Was there a single one among us who didn't take on the names of our heroes, and act like them? Take Sosthène, for example, a muscular young man from the Rex district. He worshipped Tarzan so much, he adopted his name, but we knew he wasn't the real one because every time he tried to swing from branch to branch he fell and limped for the next three days. Zembla was much more like us, we found his name 'very African', compared to Tintin or Blek le Roc. We were particularly fond of his friends Rasmus, Pétoulet, Tabuka, Satanas, Bwana and especially Yéyé, a black child, like us. We didn't want anything bad to happen to him. The useless conjuror, Rasmus, had us doubled up with laughter. When his magic tricks went wrong we felt sorry for him and hoped that some day or other he would become the greatest magician in the world. Many of Zembla's friends were animals – which we found reassuring, as we believed animals had souls, that they were the origin of the human species, and that each of us had an animal double hidden somewhere in the forest. We were amazed by Pétoulet, the kangaroo, as there was no such animal in our country, it came from a continent we couldn't find on the world map pinned up on the classroom wall. For this reason Pétoulet was our favourite of all the wild creatures. The lion and the panther were carnivores. Pétoulet, on the other hand, was what nowadays would be called a vegetarian. But he still had to go hunting, to feed all Zembla's animal friends, especially that greedy Satanas.

The lion, Bwana, terrified us, though he was less wicked than in our traditional stories, where he was a carnivore who ate up all the children until finally the smallest of them all, aided by the spirits of the forest, managed to slay him. The name Bwana – which featured in Tarzan too – meaning 'master' in Swahili, was not offensive to us, even though it later came to symbolise submission, domination.

I didn't realise that in the library you could read whatever you felt like reading, picking things randomly off the shelf. I worked my way through in alphabetical order, starting to read the authors of French classical literature, beginning with

'A'. Alain-Fournier was there, with *Le Grand Meaulnes*. Jean Anouilh with *Antigone*. Guillaume Apollinaire, whose only work of any interest to me was *Le Pont Mirabeau*. Similarly with Louis Aragon, I read only *Les Yeux d'Elsa* from the collection of the same title. I remember I skipped Antonin Artaud and Margue-rite Audoux, and went quickly on to Marcel Aymé and *The Wonderful Farm* – I loved the cat who could make it rain, and admired Garou-Garou, who could walk through walls. Missing out Artaud and Audoux meant I got all the more quickly on to Balzac, whose novels alone took up a huge amount of space on the shelves. At this rate – unless I missed out quite a few writers – it was going to take me a very long time to get to Zola. Every time I saw a reader with one of his books I wondered how they could have managed to read all the books in the library. I reassured myself by saying they must have cheated, that he was just showing off with the works of Zola, to impress the girls. So whenever I was alone I would get on with *The Wonderful Farm*, but the moment I spotted a girl, I'd open up *Germinal*, with the look of someone so extremely studious they've actually finished reading the entire library. If a friend came over and was surprised to see Marcel Aymé on my table, I had an answer ready to hand: 'I've finished all the books from A to Z, now I'm reading the first and the last ones again.'

Later, when I arrived in Nantes to continue my law studies, I happened to tune in one Friday evening to *Apostrophes*, a book programme chaired by Bernard Pivot. I almost leaped out of my seat when I saw that his guest was Jean Dutourd, whose *A Dog's Head* I had read, a book in which a child had a spaniel's head and big ears, which got him into all sorts of scrapes at school, during his military service and in his daily life, until in the end he met the love of his life. I turned to my French friends and said:

'I read that author in Africa!'

Surprised, one of them asked:

'Jean Dutourd? He's on the syllabus in Africa?'

'No, but he's well placed…'

'What do you mean, "well placed"?'

'In the library of the French Cultural Centre in Pointe-Noire, he comes under D, after Alphonse Daudet, Denis Diderot, Alexandre Dumas…'

'I still don't understand!'

My friends' perplexity sent me back into my shell. I didn't want to explain my adventures in detail, and we listened quietly to Dutourd, an old man with a moustache and glasses, talking enthusiastically about his most recent publication…

Farewell my concubine

My plane is tonight at eleven o' clock. I'm leaving today, Sunday, and it's so quiet that even the cars go slowly down the Avenue Général de Gaulle, though during the week this is one of the busiest streets in the town.

From my balcony I look over at the Adolphe-Sicé hospital, letting my cup of coffee go cold. Bienvenüe is still in hospital. I must go and say goodbye to her. I know she would appreciate the gesture.

A pair of amorous crows peck at each other on top of the hospital building. The more excited of the two is the rutting male. They're mating, and will make babies with plumage as dark as their own, while some of the patients, on the other hand, will leave for a country where the sun never rises. Even while I'm watching them disporting themselves, I think of all the things I haven't done, and should have done, during my stay. I should, for example, have gone to the Mont-Kamba cemetery to visit my parents' graves. It's what any son would have done. But I hadn't put it on my list of places to visit. Because Maman Pauline and Papa Roger came to me. They've been in this room with me all this time. They watch me writing, pull me up from time to time, and whisper to me what I should write down. Also, I tell myself that if I had gone to the cemetery, my other deceased relatives – my uncles, René and Albert, and my aunts, Sabine and Dorothée, among others – would have been cross with me and wouldn't have forgiven me for not going to see their graves. Another reason held me back: the deceased find it awkward when the living suddenly turn up in the garden of the supine before the actual day of remembrance, 2 November. They hate it when someone just walks into their bedrooms and they have to quickly get up and put on decent clothes to receive them...

Yesterday I didn't want to see anyone. I stayed in the apartment alone, pacing between the balcony, the living room, the bedroom. It was the day when I really got stuck into my writing. Exhausted, I dozed off, dreaming I had wings, that I flew over the forest of Mayombé as far as Les Bandas, the village where my mother had bought a huge field of manioc and maize and built a house out of clay. In my dream, Uncle Jean-Pierre Matété told me that the house and the field were still there, that I should do something about it, because Les Bandas isn't a village any more: a motorway goes there now, on the way to Brazzaville.

I woke with a start at the sound of the window, which had banged to in the wind. For a long while I sat looking at the painting on the wall: the sad lady smiled at me. At least that's how it seemed as I went up to her, as though her face was relaxing, her eyes filling with the natural light of day. Suddenly she looked just like my mother...

That evening I felt like getting drunk, to forget that I'd been trampling on the kingdom of my childhood. What would be the point, though? To be like the young man I had met in the late afternoon the day before last, in the Rex district, homeless, but apparently happy? He wanted me to take his picture, to show the whole world he lived on next to nothing, his glass was small but his own, and he was happy with that.

'I'm nothing, I'm everything,' he declared. 'The street is my mother. The sun is my father. What more should I ask of life?'

Now the street is everyone's mother, as is the sun. He was proud to be a child of the streets. And a child, too, of the sun.

'My name's Yannick. I want to be your little brother… Will you have me?'

I hesitated, finding his request a bit weird. In the end I said yes. Why would I say no, after all, when up till now I had been making up my own brothers and sisters in cardboard cut-outs?

That evening I put together my few belongings. Most precious were the pages of this notebook that I'd crumpled up and thrown in the bin in the kitchen. There were others, too, all around me, and I couldn't possibly reread them all. I could just imagine the look on the faces of the customs people at Pointe-Noire, when they opened my suitcase and found a whole load of paper. They'd think I was some kind of mental retard or a spy who was concealing vital information among all this mess. Would they suspect that there was a bit of their own lives in these crossings-out, these indecisions of writing?

I also packed the self-published books which had been given me by various local authors. I promised myself I would read them in Europe or America. There is always something enriching in the suffering of a creator who hopes his bottle thrown into the sea will one day reach its destination. The knowledge that their work would be on that plane with me made them both glad and anxious. Glad because, for a short while, I would be carrying the burden of their obsessions. But they also dreaded me reading it, because I had already told them that many books are not made to travel, and disintegrate as soon as the plane crosses over borders. These are books that can be read only in the place where they were written. They have no passport, can't tolerate changes in climate, and discover that summer in the north is less warm than a heat wave in the tropics…

The taxi driver puts my luggage in the boot while my girlfriend takes a few last photos of the area around the French Institute and dives into the taxi.

I look once more at the street lamps on the Avenue Général de Gaulle. The yellowish light, and the insects buzzing round, make my head spin. When it comes down to it, this town and I are in an open relationship, she is my concubine, and this time I seem to be saying adieu. I'm so moved, I shed not one single tear.

As I finally get into the taxi, I wonder, as I always do, and as I always will: when will I return to Pointe-Noire again?

Postscript

On 15 July 2012, I had a phone call from Gilbert to say my grandmother, Hélène, had just died. Exactly three weeks to the day after my departure from Pointe-Noire. So the old lady wasn't wrong: she had waited to be delivered by a white woman. Along with the other members of the family, I made my contribution, sending a sum of money by Western Union, which Gilbert handed over to her widower, Old Joseph, before witnesses. Because so many families have torn each other apart over that. People always exaggerate the amount of money sent by a relative living abroad. When Gilbert called me, he put on the loudspeaker:

'Cousin, I've got ten people sitting round me, including Uncle Mompéro and Grand Poupy. Can you tell us yourself how much you just sent for Grandmother Hélène's funeral?...'

I told him, and he repeated the amount out loud so that the others wouldn't bring a case against him. When I hung up, I saw again the old lady, rigid under her mosquito net, and her hand gripping me as though holding on to life itself...

I've spoken to Gilbert again on the telephone. Bienvenüe left the Adolphe-Sicé hospital the very day after Grandmother Hélène's funeral. He was like a man who has just pulled off a victory:

'Because you know, cousin, when she was in that hospital, a bit of me was in there with her! We shared the same womb, we wallowed in the same amniotic fluid! You can tell me the truth now. You were a bit scared too, weren't you? That's why you didn't go and visit her, when you were living opposite! I do understand – you know it's the first time a member of our family has been in hospital, in that room, Room One, and come out alive? My father – your uncle – he died in that room, didn't he? I was scared, I prayed every day. I was even tempted to go and pray in the pentecostal church of the New Jerusalem – just goes to show!'